Digital Captives

Helping Schools Strike a Balance Between the Human and the Hardware

Dr. Francisco Rodriguez

Dr. Donna Smith

Dr. Gene Tavernetti

Every effort has been made to trace all copyright holders, but if any have been inadvertently overlooked, the Publishers will be pleased to make the necessary arrangements at the first opportunity.

Although every effort has been made to ensure that website addresses are correct at time of going to press, Schools Next Press cannot be held responsible for the content of any website mentioned in this book. It is sometimes possible to find a relocated web page by typing in the address of the home page for a website in the URL window of your browser.

ISBN: 979-8-9947286-0-4

First published in 2026 by:

Schools Next Press
16654 Soledad Canyon Road
#249
Santa Clarita, CA 91387
www.schoolsnext.org

This book is dedicated to teachers who teach, and to children
who need to be taught.

"We can, whenever and wherever we choose, successfully teach all children whose schooling is of interest to us. We already know more than we need to do this. Whether we do it or not must finally depend on how we feel about the fact that we have not done it so far."

Ronald Edmonds
American educator
1935-1983

Table of Contents

Prologue

Setting:
Emergency School Board Meeting of Fictional
Irving School District*
Upstate New York
Late December 2014

Nick Vedder, Board President: "This meeting of the Irving School District is called to order. The only item on the agenda is the emergency resolution to consider applying for the new E-rate funds being distributed by the Federal Communications Commission. We will hear from Superintendent Van Bummel on the pros and cons of applying for these funds and determine whether to proceed."

Superintendent Van Bummel: "Thank you, Board President Vedder and board members. I'd like to start by saying, if I may be so bold, there really are no cons to applying for these funds; it's all positives. The FCC approved a large increase in the E-Rate funding last week. We are in a really strong position to secure funds that will help us bring increased bandwidth to every classroom, secure additional hardware, and help us narrow the digital divide with districts that are a few years ahead of us.

"All of you read the newspaper and know how vital it is that our students have high-speed access to the internet to develop the skills of the future. Our community is feeling that pressure as well. We have lost 18 students in this last year whose families decided to move them to the bigger districts in Albany, because they fear we can't compete digitally and are being left behind. I fear we are being left behind as well.

"As you know, the Common Core Standards will be assessed digitally starting in a couple of years. If our students don't spend time on screen, with keyboards, working with the tools they'll need on that assessment, they're going to do poorly. That might cause more families to leave. In a small district like ours,

1

losing just a few more students means that we will have to cut a classroom teaching position, and nobody wants that.

"These funds are basically free. Mandated contributions from the large tech and internet companies fund the E-rate. As a small rural district, we are first in line to get everything we need in terms of connectivity. Every day, I get phone calls and emails from software companies that offer amazing individualized platforms. Every student can have their own login and proceed at their own pace, based on where they are. The kids love being on the devices- they're such a novelty- so that learning is fun. They help teachers with planning and engagement tools. The desktops and laptops that we have are too expensive and cumbersome, though, and our Wi-Fi is too spotty to be able to run these new platforms and programs broadly. We need broadband so that every classroom can connect multiple computers at the same time. Once we can do that, it will also allow us to move to those new laptops from Google that are much less expensive. We can buy a whole classroom cart of their Chromebooks for about the cost of 5 quality laptops with more memory. The Chromebooks don't need the same amount of memory to access applications off the net. We can have a screen in front of every student no later than 2016.

"It's a win-win, and we heartily recommend that the board adopt the resolution to let us get after it. Thank you."

President Vedder: "Thank you, Superintendent Van Bummel. That was very informative. This sounds wonderful to me. If we have no questions from the board members, we can go right to the vote. If I heard you correctly, there's no catch, and all we need to do is contract with the companies that will run the cable and set up our classrooms, is that right?"

Superintendent Van Bummel: "That's correct. The tech companies realize that our children will need these tools to be successful in the future, and so they're willing partners. They want to help our students access and use 21st-century skills. For example, some of the largest companies are helping to fund the Common Core digital assessments."

President Vedder: "I love it, love it. The tech giants are being good civic citizens. What's not to like? I'd like to call for the vote..."

Board member Gardenier: (interrupting) "Actually, I have a couple of questions. Mr. Van Bummel—Everything sounds great, but I want to be sure- will our teachers receive training before they need to implement these new programs that you were talking about?"

Superintendent Van Bummel: "Oh, of course, of course. As you know, we have tight controls on what makes its way into the classrooms. We want to be sure that teachers are successful and that we give them all the necessary support. I think these new programs will really send the message to our teachers how much we support them, and to our community that we value the skills they value, and will do everything to develop citizens for the 21st century."

Board member Gardenier: "Wonderful, thank you. A few more quick questions—are these programs effective? How do we know? You mentioned that students will work at their own pace based on where they are. My question is, when will they catch up? The push for so long has been to not leave any children behind, and it seems like these programs might do exactly that."

Superintendent Van Bummel: "Everything that the software companies send us shows that the students make great progress and feel more confident. And as I said, they love being on the devices and the programs. One of the programs, as they accumulate more lessons, they get to drive a little car around a track and get tokens. There's a token leaderboard, and all of the students are competing with each other. So it's like a game. They're learning, and they don't even know they're learning.

"And it allows for smaller groups, so that teachers can help those struggling students catch up. Incredible tools, incredible..."

Board member Gardenier: "Yes, they sound great, but what about No Child Left Behind?"

Superintendent Van Bummel: "NCLB is up for reauthorization. Members of one party don't want the federal government involved in education, so they are more than happy to let it die, even though it came from their own party's administration. And the current administration's party is deeply tied to the national teachers' associations, which are also against NCLB. NCLB is going away, and what will take its place is something that gives more discretion at the state level, prioritizes individualized learning, and takes advantage of these technological tools. We want to get out in front of that."

Board President Vedder: (interjecting as Ms. Gardenier opens her mouth to speak) "I think we are ready to move to a vote. I'm sure that all of your concerns will be handled as they come, Ms. Gardenier. We will take it gradually and intelligently, but as the superintendent said, we need to move fast to keep up with the districts around us. I saw an article in the Albany Times Union a couple of months ago.[1] One of the school leaders interviewed said that in 20 years, what is that, 2034, people will look back at how schools reacted when the world changed, and they were talking about this exact thing. Will we jump on board, or be left on the side of the road? We don't want to be the school district that was left behind. Call for the vote, please."

Board Secretary: "All in favor?"

Members: (except Gardenier) "Aye!"

Board Secretary: "Opposed?"

No response.

Board Secretary: "Board member Gardenier?"

Gardenier: (pausing) "Abstain."

Board Secretary: "Resolution passes 4-0 with one abstention."

Board President Vedder: (rolls eyes) "Great, thank you all, thank you for coming out in the middle of the holiday season. As Mr. Van Bummel said, the e-rate increase just happened last week, so we needed to jump on this, need to act fast. The meeting is adjourned. Thank you, Superintendent Van Bummel. Happy holidays to everyone. I'm really excited about this. What could go wrong?"

Gavel

Introduction

"It is so much our servant that it would seem churlish to notice that it is also our master."
-**Nicholas Carr**[1]

Digital Natives or Digital Captives

In the early part of this century, when it became evident that digital technology and the internet were going to play a major role in schools, educators—including all the authors—would chuckle and nod knowledgeably. A popular refrain was "well, we're digital immigrants, but the kids are going to be digital natives." Students would, in this view, grow up with the technology in a healthy way, learning it as naturally as the child of immigrants learns the language of the new place.

What we were not counting on was the speed of the change and how it would envelop everything we do so quickly. At the turn of the century, most of us were still using dial-up to access the Internet.[2] It was something you went to, not something that surrounded you. An early broadband commercial in 1999 promised "Every movie ever made, in any language, day or night," which seemed so fanciful given that most households still had to decide whether to be on a phone call or the World Wide Web because the same phone line brought both into your home.[3] Of course, within a few years, Netflix would start its streaming service, able to deliver almost any movie ever made, day or night.

In schools, the early part of the century, say 2000 to 2005, saw an increase in technology as a wonderful tool that would add to the educational experience, but it wasn't something that replaced the nuts and bolts of human interaction, inside or outside of the classroom. Early adopters talked about the ability to have students go on "virtual field trips," or create educational videos or other media for presentations. It was the dawn of an optimistic time.

The digital rush came so fast though and became so ubiquitous—
YouTube, smartphones, likes and re-tweets, social media, millions
of offerings in app stores, push notifications, infinite scroll,
individualized feeds curated by algorithms, short, addictive videos,
user-created content—that it can be said that in one generation
our students went from being digital natives to being digital
captives.

The rush overwhelmed adults' ability to gradually assimilate
the new offerings, leaving us with a sense of uneven footing, of
displacement, with a fear of missing out as the world sped up. The
impact on children growing up in this new world with no prior
analog experience to use as an anchor was even greater.

An early book on the impact, by Nicholas Carr, *The Shallows:
What the Internet is Doing to Our Brains*, sounded the alarm.[4]
The digital tools that were to make our lives easier, so that we
could concentrate on deep thinking, were instead making us
intellectually lazier. The ability to read deeply and linearly,
sustain focus, memorize, calculate, and navigate a map was being
delegated to our devices and creating new neural pathways that
took shortcuts around long-established mental patterns.

Researchers whose work we learn from and rely on—Johann Hari,
Jonathan Haidt, Jean Twenge, and others—have written about the
impact of these new technologies on children and society. While
their work touches on schools, they are writing as well about
social-emotional and mental health, increases in depression and
anxiety, loneliness, and addictive behaviors. They write about the
lack of connectedness and the loss of social networks, of free play,
of communication.

This book looks at the same issues through a different lens—the
impact that this digital revolution has had on schools and on
classroom instruction specifically. It is our position that it isn't
just the children who are digital captives, but that schools and
the whole educational system have become captive as well. Many
school districts and educators have turned over the crucial act
of teaching to screens, to individualized platforms that promise
to tailor instruction to each student's needs. Less obvious in the
equation is the opportunity cost: what is being displaced?

While the role of the COVID-19 pandemic cannot be underestimated in this development, it also doesn't bear the sole blame. Decision-making by educators at every level of the system, starting in the early 2010s—from the federal government to local school boards—promoted this trend, which has resulted in children in some schools receiving more than half of their daily instruction through a laptop, in isolation from their peers.

The slow but accelerating burn of having every child on a screen for the majority of the day became a necessity during the pandemic. Remote learning was the lifeline during a time of uncertainty and fear. The authors—all of whom were working in schools in 2020—understand the necessity of the actions taken.

The problem was that in an instant, education went from being a transformational activity, where children and communities were enriched by the interactions inherent in schools, to a transactional activity, where the transmission of content became the main objective.

And once every child had a screen in their hands, it became difficult to put that genie back in the bottle. Different digital curriculum platforms, technology giants, and educational publishing conglomerates accelerated their competition for prime cuts of the most valuable resources schools have—captive students and the accompanying flood of federal funds meant to help address learning loss.

It is our position that schools generally didn't take what was learned about digital instruction during the pandemic and apply it after the pandemic to establish a new balance of in-person instruction and interaction augmented by technological aids. Instead, with the help of eager vendors and with the intent of supporting beleaguered educators mentally exhausted from the pandemic, digital instruction morphed into a replacement for human interaction in many classrooms.

> Education went from being a transformational activity, where children and communities were enriched by the interactions inherent in schools, to a transactional activity, where the transmission of content became the main objective.

Technology could have been used sparingly and intentionally upon return to more normal operations. Technology could have been a useful tool integrated into the greater ecosphere of a healthy learning environment with student-student interaction, student-adult interaction, purposeful and inspiring adult-led instruction, development of durable life skills, and a vibrant community. But school systems themselves became captives to the digital tools, in the same way that individuals had in the preceding two decades. And the devil's bargain is that every minute of something new displaces a minute of something else. The school day and year have gotten no longer, and the various digital learning platforms are not going to easily give up the real estate they have won.

And school systems and the vendors they contracted with could not have transformed what the school day looks like in many districts without the tacit agreement of parents and the surrounding community. With many adults being digital captives themselves, it wasn't easy to notice the changes to what the school experience looked like for children.

The work of Haidt, Hari, Carr, Twenge, and the others speaks to the changes that are going on in our brains the longer we are on screens of isolation, whether our addiction be short videos, checking emails, infinite scrolls, gambling, or playing video games. Linking the impact of this ubiquitous screen time to student behavior in the classrooms is only now starting to gain attention. Teachers are noting that what were once aberrant behaviors are becoming the norm. Teachers are seeing students running out of classrooms, striking adults, and not being able to communicate their thoughts and emotions. Teachers notice the difference, because they see more of it on a daily basis: dysregulated behavior, shorter attention spans, more fragmented focus, inability to sustain attention, poor fine motor skills, student isolation, poorer communication, and an inability to work together.

A Department of Education report titled Supporting Child and Student Social, Emotional, Behavioral, and Mental Health Needs details how, even prior to the pandemic, children and youth in the US were demonstrating escalating mental health needs.[5] Many students are coming to school with their brains wired

differently than children even ten years ago.[6] A 2-or 3-year-old in
2015, whether in a shopping cart at a grocery store or at a table
in a restaurant, experienced all of the sights, sounds, and smells
of their environment. They experienced the greetings, the quiet
negotiations of space, and taking turns. They experienced the
colors and distractions going on all around them, literally helping
them develop executive function as they made their way down the
cookie aisle, or as they colored and completed connect-a-dots on
paper menus at the restaurant table. In 2026, a 2-or 3-year-old in
a shopping cart or at a restaurant is just as likely to be glued to a
screen, entranced by what is going on 6 inches from their face. A
child who never has to contend with what NOT to focus on, who
has not trained their brain "focus on this, not that," will have a
much more difficult time when they enter kindergarten and are
required to do so.

The average adult now spends between seven and nine hours per
day on screens.[7] We don't all work in offices. Where did those
hours come from? Answering that question may help with the
realization that the exact same opportunity cost is taking its toll
on children: if they are staring at a screen for two or three hours at
school and four or five hours at home, what is being lost?

Participation by children of all ages in outside sports and activities
has diminished.[8] Church and civic participation by adults has
diminished as well. Addressing the impacts of an over-saturation
of screen time can't be work that is only done in schools when
the pressure to not miss out on the latest post is so strong, and
when social media companies are vying for viewing minutes in the
7,000-plus hours per year that students are not in school.

The solutions will require a whole community effort. It will take
brave, perceptive school leaders and parents to address it. During
the pandemic, children's time on screens went up and never went
back down, and the same can be said for adults.[9] Will adults be
able to break out of their digital captivity long enough to address
these issues? The concern of many is that adults are also so
distracted that we may not even realize the scope of the problem.

The answers that are needed are not going to be found where we
are looking—on screens. The answer is not necessarily to turn

back the clock, but to blend the best of what schools offered before the digital rush- that is, quality human instruction, personal connections, learning as a social activity- with the tools and amazing capacities available now through technology.

There is a different path forward than what most of us succumb to daily: more time spent on screens, both in school and out, accessing different music, videos, posts, and news based on our individualized algorithms, together, but not. There is also a different path forward for schools than continuing to add screen minutes to students' days, without consideration to what is being lost. This book is an attempt to work with schools on regaining that balance.

Our Process and Learning Curve

When we started research on this project in early 2024, bringing together career educators from literally the four corners of the United States, our focus was on artificial intelligence (AI) and its current state and future place in schools. Our concern was that schools were not ready to thoughtfully integrate artificial intelligence into daily operations, but nevertheless were rushing to make investments based on the promises of a still-developing technology, and of fears of being left behind, much like a decade earlier.

Our initial conversations with educators focused on how to use AI to support tasks from lesson planning, grading, and providing feedback on essays, to increased efficiency in everything from contacting parents to planning better bus routes. As the conversations turned to impacts at the student level, the tone changed from one of optimism to fear, of how to prevent students from accessing the same technology to "cheat."

Students—digital natives—had equal access to chatbots, however, and more flexible ways of adapting them to suit their needs at a speed that outpaced schools' ability to monitor use. For every student who was using AI intelligently to help them plan for a mid-term by preparing a mock quiz and providing corrective feedback, or for help in organizing data for a report, the perception is that there were ten who were using it to write their essays for them. The majority opinion in those conversations seemed to be how to use AI at the adult level, while keeping it from being used at the student level, even as it gained a growing hold in society.

Much hyped announcements, such as that of a multi-million-dollar investment by the Los Angeles Unified School District in its AI chatbot, followed by less publicized collapses of those initiatives, accelerated the sense that districts were rushing into a future they were not ready to navigate.[10] Many districts, and individual schools, were pursuing piecemeal approaches to AI in the absence of a vision of how to integrate the technology, so our conversations turned to forward-looking questions: what would schools look like in 5 or 10 years, with full implementation? What would a school day look like? What would a school building look like?

That work began at the district administration level, in conversations with superintendents, assistant superintendents of educational services, and directors of technology and instruction. Those talks focused on where these school leaders saw their districts in 2030 and beyond, specifically with regard to artificial intelligence and its promise to revolutionize everything, including teaching and learning. We were surprised, however, when a number of the conversations took a turn towards "2030? I'm trying to make it to next Thursday!" Administrators described a level of fatigue similar to 2020 and 2021 during the pandemic. A fatigue driven by staff shortages, chronic absenteeism, and more extreme student behaviors than they'd previously dealt with regularly. A fatigue driven by unprecedented antagonism from parents and by carryover mistrust from pandemic-related decision-making. It seemed like many that we spoke to were focused more on survival than on forward-looking decision-making. And this was happening even as digital tools took an ever-greater slice of the six-hour instructional day in district after district.

From our various vantage points working in schools, we could each tell from our over thirty years of experience in the profession that "kids" from four to twenty were acting differently. From assimilating to the expectations of school in the early grades, to interacting with each other and demonstrating mental health concerns at ever younger ages, to a distinct lack of self-awareness, eye contact, or even possession of a driver's license from college-aged students applying to work in our tutoring programs, students seemed impacted in ways that went beyond pandemic-related causes. Leaning heavily on *The Anxious Generation, Stolen Focus,* and earlier works like *Amusing Ourselves to Death* by Neil Postman, we came to believe that student issues stemmed as much from digital use and distraction outside of school as they did from lingering pandemic fallout.

At that point, our work turned away from the down-the-line threat and promise of artificial intelligence, to the immediate issues plaguing schools, and the book morphed from being a book about AI use in schools, to a book about the use of technology already in place in schools and its possible overuse and potential impact on students.

We developed the brilliant theory that children were simply on screens too much and that "detoxing" incoming kindergartners by taking them off screens would be a great step in the right direction. When we interviewed a group of district instructional technology coaches, however, we were told "that's a terrible idea. There are teachers in the early primary grades who are doing a wonderful job with technology. They use it in a targeted way, they use the data, and they use it to facilitate small group instruction. You're going to punish them because of what is happening at home before the age of five, and by administrators who keep adopting more platforms because they saw them at a conference. You need to start by talking to parents, then to the administrators."

That conversation was a critical step in the realization that the problem had more layers than we'd imagined.

The critical mental health concerns voiced by Haidt and Twenge were braided with the lack of connectedness described by Carr, and the fragmented thinking that concerned Hari, but at the school and classroom level, they were more than that. Crucial learning-how-to-learn skills were being compromised. Skills such as learning to shift and lock in focus, to memorize multi-step directions, and to sustain attention for more than a few minutes—a lot of that negative impact was happening before a child ever set foot in kindergarten.

That conversation was also critical in differentiating the impact of phones from that of classroom screens and tablets. Although the traits of shorter attention spans, fragmented focus, isolation, and non-linear reading are correlated with the use of all devices, we realized that we needed to define exactly which technology we were talking about. As parents and citizens, we are concerned about the impacts of phones and social media. As educators, though, our concern is primarily with the scattershot implementation of classroom-based technology, which has separated students from their teachers, in particular, the individualized learning platforms that students spend so much of their day on, not interacting with each other.

The deeper we dug both in the research and in interviews and conversations with more than three dozen educators from diverse settings across the country, the more that the correlation became obvious: students' ability to get along, communicate their reasoning and emotions, to focus and be interested in novel learning, started decreasing about the same time as technology hardware became ubiquitous in classrooms (and smart phones at home and in backpacks and pockets). It accelerated with the pandemic-related school closures that introduced learning through a screen en masse. And it exploded when personalized digital platforms started to promise distressed educators, "If students could just spend x minutes on this platform per day, they should be able to achieve y growth."

Why This Work? Why Now?

Public education in the United States is at an inflection point. Enrollment in mainstream public schools, defined here as traditional brick and mortar "neighborhood" schools, has declined since the pandemic, especially among groups that have more social mobility and higher levels of educational attainment.[11] Teacher interviews and research show a high level of job dissatisfaction, with more leaving the profession than coming in, creating a downward spiral of larger class sizes taught by less experienced teachers.[12]

In this environment, it is not difficult to understand why school leaders have turned to screens as a primary teaching tool. It is more difficult to say that the results have been positive and that the opportunity cost has been worth it. Comparing students from 2014 and 2024, for example, as we did in two dozen interviews with classroom teachers who were teaching similar grade levels and in similar demographics during both time periods, one is hard pressed to find any who report increased attention span, better social interactions, improved cognitive processes, more independent student behavior, and greater independence and resilience. As a matter of fact, the teachers we interviewed all reported the opposite.

And the timing is critical because, as students progress further in the grade span, not developing skills that build on each other, each year brings a school experience that is more imbalanced and less personal. Students instead delegate much of their learning to search engines and AI, in the same way that much of their instruction has been delegated to screens.

School districts that can step back and recognize this imbalance will spend time developing the following fundamental understandings with all their constituent groups:

» Affirm that time with children is the most important resource schools have, and that current technology practices have diminished the time available for the most fundamental relationships in schools, the one between teacher and students, and the one between students and their peers.
» Adopt as a core value the belief that learning is a social activity best done in collaboration with others, and have that value threaded throughout its instructional vision.
» Develop a district-wide understanding of the learning process—how the brain creates neural pathways that reinforce key skills and learning, both intellectual and social—and that how students spend their time can either help or hinder that process.

» Realize that there are no panaceas or magic bullets, regardless of what digital curriculum companies promise, that "neomania"—the adoption of anything new because it is new—is a path towards fragmented implementation, a mile wide and an inch deep.

» Harness the incredible power that technology has to augment teaching and learning, rather than replace it.

The education of children has always been difficult, arduous work, putting one building block in place on top of another. Today, the education of children in an environment that has prioritized instant gratification, rapid-fire attention switching, diminished attention spans, and gamification is heroic, almost Sisyphean work.

It feels like gravity is working against educators, and it might feel like the best response is to do the same in schools: to put screens in front of students, to teach through games, to give in to the diminished attention spans. But playing that out, where does it lead? Where will students learn

And the timing is critical because, as students progress further in the grade span, not developing skills that build on each other, each year brings a school experience that is more imbalanced and less personal.

to use academic language, to read linearly and deeply, to work through complex multi-step problems, to learn content they would not otherwise access through their social media, if not in school? Where, if not in school, will they learn to read great works that on their own they might say "TLDR" (Too long, didn't read) to, an acronym that captures the ethos of shorter is better more appropriately than just about any other Generation Z saying?

Education has literally become a battle for student minds, between forces that, for profit, are okay with sacrificing student attention span, ability to focus and communicate cogently, and those that recognize that this is happening and take steps to pull back from a downward instructional spiral.

Two studies and one quote from Johann Hari's *Stolen Focus* encapsulate what we argue. In one study, the median amount of time students focused on any one thing was nineteen seconds. In the second study, adults working in an office weren't much better: the average adult stayed on task for about three minutes.[13]

Those numbers are scary. The scariest is the gap between young adults at 19 seconds and older adults at three minutes. The adults who stayed on task for three minutes presumably grew up in a more analog world, one where attention was not as compromised. They actually learned to direct their brains to focus, from the time they were in a shopping cart glancing around, to sitting and listening to their teacher read a story aloud, to themselves reading books left to right. How long will today's college students, trained in a world where switching attention rapidly is what they practice, both in school and out, be able to focus in 10 years, when they are the ones working in an office? And what of today's second grader? What will become of her?

To paraphrase one of Hari's interviews, when Hari asked a researcher what he would do if he were in charge of the world and wanted to ruin people's ability to pay attention. The answer was "Probably about what our society is doing."[14]

Will our schools say differently?

Chapter 1
A Tale of Two Classrooms

"There's a dark little joke exchanged by educators with a dissident streak: Rip Van Winkle awakens in the 21st century after a hundred-year snooze and is, of course, utterly bewildered by what he sees... Airports, hospitals, shopping malls- every place Rip goes just baffles him. But when he finally walks into a schoolroom, the old man knows exactly where he is. "This is a school," he declares," We used to have these back in 1906. Only now the blackboards are green."[1]
How to Bring Our Schools Out of the 20th Century Time Magazine, December 10, 2006

2014

Imagine that Rip doesn't go back to sleep in the Catskills and instead stays awake until 2014. He sees a rapid evolution of what is going on in classrooms: the laser disc players and Macintosh Classics and bulky iMac G3s that were avant-garde just a few years before are replaced by sleek, individualized Chromebooks and tablets at technology centers in every classroom. The younger teachers and the techie ones walk into class looking at their smartphones, starting maybe with a Blackberry but then graduating to the newest iPhone or Android. The green chalkboards and dry-erase whiteboards are replaced by "smart boards": giant screens that can project the internet and be manipulated by touch. Students are astounded by the technology making its way into their classroom, but they can't know the extent of the sea change from just ten years earlier.

Only Rip and the educators born before about 1980 know that something is changing, something exciting is happening. While the classroom still looks similar with daily, personal instruction, collaborative groups, print-rich environments, puzzles, songs, picture books, and art supplies, teachers are also learning to use technology and the internet as a tool in their arsenal. In primary classrooms, there are still "listening centers" and places for students to practice fine motor skills and writing. But there are also shared tablets and Chromebooks where students can listen to stories or play games. In the middle grades, students are being introduced to personalized platforms that teach adaptive standards-based lessons guided by pre-assessments that determine students' strengths and areas of needed growth. At the high school level, using the internet to conduct research, word processing, compiling spreadsheets, and producing slide decks has gone from an exception to the expectation.

Schools have evolved and found a balance. Professional learning communities use advanced data analysis to help target curriculum and instruction. Teachers teach and use technology as a supplement and an aid. Students collaborate while learning not just the content of the curriculum standards, but also the technological tools they will need to succeed in the future. Standardized state assessments, long the nightmare made of bubbling in with number 2 pencils, are migrating to computer-based, adaptive assessments that respond to how students are doing, more quickly and accurately determining their performance level on the recently adopted Common Core Standards. The educational system is finally moving towards the 21st Century, and technology is promising to support by serving as a great equalizer— helping students close achievement gaps through individualized instruction and helping lighten the loads on teachers.

Rip is happy.

It is a fleeting moment where the optimism of how technology can improve the schooling experience, both for students and their teachers, brims with possibilities, with positivity. Unfortunately, the earliest young adopters of screens, right about the same time, start to show that everything is not positive.

As one researcher put it, the kids are "not all right," being "on the brink of the worst mental-health crisis in decades." So even as schools raced to adopt more technology as a panacea, espe-cially individualized platforms which by their nature isolate students and separate them socially, if not physically, from the student sitting next to them, the same students started to show signs of distress, demonstrating marked increases in anxiety, depression and sleep deprivation associated with an explosion in phone and social media usage outside of school.

Consider these statistics from Nicholas Carr's *Superbloom:*

» The percentage of teens in the US experiencing a major episode of depression doubled between 2010 and 2019
» Non-fatal self-harm increased by more than 35% over the same period
» Suicide attempt rates increased dramatically for both younger and older children[3]

Carr cited Jean Twenge's book *Generations,* which showed that it was "the rapid growth in digital media use that exhibits by far the strongest and most consistent association with the surge in psychological problems."[4]

> "It's not an exaggeration to describe iGen as being on the brink of the worst mental-health crisis in decades. Much of this deterioration can be traced to their phones."
>
> "Have Smartphones Destroyed a Generation?"
> *The Atlantic*
> September 2017
> Jean Twenge

The years immediately around 2014 serve as a hinge in the time frame of the early 2010s to the period right before the start of the COVID-19 pandemic. It is when smartphones overtook previous types of phones for most Americans, and social media became ubiquitous.[5] Jonathan Haidt called out this period as the time when youth mental health issues, ranging from major depression to anxiety, alienation in school, and other illnesses, suddenly spiked.[6]

Johann Hari similarly referred to it as a time when information distribution greatly sped up, lending the environment a sense of speed, overtaking people and institutions, and the feeling that no one wanted to be left behind and out of the loop—from anxious teenagers to school district administrators to school board presidents.[7]

It was precisely in this period that schools were poised to jump into a surge in digital media use fueled by a confluence of three distinct but related factors:

1. The replacement of the No Child Left Behind federal education policy with the Every Student Succeeds Act, which advocated for individuals to learn at their own pace.
2. The push by the Obama Administration to increase bandwidth access to poor and rural areas, which resulted in massively increased funding through the Federal Communications Commission E-Rate program.
3. The full implementation of Common Core Assessments- the Smarter Balanced Assessment Consortium (SBAC) and the Partnership for Assessment of Readiness for College and Careers (PARCC)- which went to an almost completely computer-based format between 2014 and 2016.

The debate over the re-authorization of the 2001 No Child Left Behind Act, with the Obama administration determined to end some of the more stringent federal requirements, resulted in the passage of the Every Student Succeeds Act (ESSA) in 2015. The ESSA deemphasized standardized testing and allowed for more flexible, personal approaches to education, recognizing "the importance of tailoring education to meet individual student needs."[8]

If the Rip Van Winkle allegory is used frequently in education, an even more common literary device is the metaphor of the pendulum, and the idea that for every swing in one direction of policy or practice, there will be a corresponding, reactionary swing in the other direction. And, true to the analogy, educators responded in kind.

They swung away from pacing guides and common assessments to meet the "tailoring" curriculum in the most readily available way possible: digital platforms that promised to meet every child's individual needs.

The technological hardware of the future was already in place in classrooms across the country: smart boards, Chromebooks, tablets, and platforms designed to teach curriculum standards. What was not in place yet was the personalized, tailored instruction called for by ESSA. Software platforms deftly pivoted their marketing and raced to be the most individualized and be at the forefront of school districts' move away from the unpopular, defunct No Child Left Behind. The period between the start of 2016 and the end of 2019 showed a more than 50 percent increase in technology spending, specifically linked to digital curricula.[9]

The stars had aligned to make software platforms and digital curriculum the dominant feature of American classrooms. All that was needed was a good crisis to really cement them in place.

THE COVID-19 PANDEMIC 2020-2022

The effects of the pandemic reverberated for years after it arrived in the US in early 2020. It is reasonable to argue that schools did not quickly regain their footing even as the health crisis subsided, with changes in instructional delivery, a student exodus from mainstream public schools, chronic absenteeism, and large-scale educator retirements.

The first reaction, completely understandable, to try and keep education as central to students' lives as it had been prior to schools shuttering, was to rapidly dive into remote learning. This single step had an unforeseen consequence that has become a dominant feature in many classrooms across the country: education through a screen.

The pandemic accelerated tremendous shifts in the American educational system, decoupling the concept of schooling from school buildings.

When school buildings closed, the shift redefined how we think about teaching and learning, how our teachers teach, and how our students learn. Learning became a transactional process, with content to be learned as the end benefit, rather than a transformational one, in which content is learned while students are also learning how to collaborate, communicate, work together, think critically, persuade others, interact, disagree, and so many other durable life skills.

What was supposed to be a temporary solution became permanent for some, as enrollment in online charter and virtual schools increased post-pandemic, drawing students away from mainstream public schools. In the 10-year span between 2013 and 2023, enrollment in virtual schools expanded by more than 350,000 students.[10] Further, almost 1.2 million students in U.S. public schools did not return following the pandemic. While two-thirds of these students transitioned to homeschooling or private schools, where the remaining third went is unknown.[11] Chronic absenteeism also grew post-pandemic, with "around 19% of students missing 10% or more school days during the 2023-24 school year."[12]

POST PANDEMIC DECISION MAKING

School leaders experienced the pandemic like everyone else, suffering from the same anxiety, uncertainty, and lack of direction as the rest of us, all while having to deal with massive organizations at the epicenter of controversial decision-making that impacted the lives of millions of people daily. Furthermore, they were now in charge of one of the institutions whose value, unquestioned in years past, was suddenly up for debate. If students could achieve the same diploma and learning at home during the pandemic, what was the need for the massive investment in schools at the public level? And at the individual family level, what was the need to send their child to a brick-and-mortar school, to possibly catch a virus, be bullied, or worse?

As states staggered out of the pandemic and school closures, school leaders had to make in-the-moment decisions about technology purchases worth millions of dollars of disappearing time-sensitive pandemic-related funding, without the time to be strategic or reflective. The result was the accelerated adoption of digital tools and online learning platforms, haphazardly in many cases, trying to match the offerings of online virtual schools.

In 2022 U.S. K-12 schools and districts spent $38.2 billion on technology, including hardware, software, and digital curriculum, an increase of $2.4 billion from the previous year. The spending on digital curriculum alone jumped from $13.1 billion to $15.1 billion.[13]

2024

Students went from spending an average of less than 30 minutes per day working on their own on individualized platforms in 2014, to more than 3 hours per day in 2024.[14] When this is added to the screen time that students are experiencing while away from school, there is no question that students are generally using significantly more screen time than is recommended for any school-age group.

The concomitant social-emotional, mental, and physical impacts are numerous and well documented—from anxiety to depression to lack of adequate sleep.[15] We are not suggesting that the school-based screen time is a cause for these ills, but school-based screen time is not without fault. Rather, school-based screen time literally upended not just the teaching and learning process, but much of what made schools and classrooms transformational places, and piled on top of the hours already spent on devices outside of school.

Reflective educational leaders must ask themselves where the hours that students are spending on screens, mostly in isolation, are coming from, and to what end. As students move from one learning platform for math to another for English Language Arts and reading, to a third for science (in some elementary schools, accounting for up to four instructional hours in a six-hour day)[16] what has been lost?

We have been in schools where, following a cohort of students at the secondary level for the day, students go from one online digital platform assignment completed in isolation in period one, to another one in period two, another in period three, and so on. Students can go half a day or more without speaking to another student in class, and in schools where personal cell phones and devices are allowed, that silence extends to what formerly was the most boisterous time—lunch time, passing period, the precious minutes in the classroom before the bell rang and the class period started—as students instead scroll through infinite content in isolated silos.

What is lost is socialization, communication, collaboration, and team-building- in many cases, exactly what employers say that young graduates need. But more important even than the jobs of the future are the learning skills not being developed today, separate from the content. In interviews with experienced teachers representing a broad range of school and district sizes, demographics, and locations, a few skills were consistently mentioned as being substantially lower than in 2014. We can think of these as "pre-content" skills that are really about the ability to learn:

» Ability to carry information in immediate working memory for more than a few seconds
» Ability to shift and maintain focus
» Task-persistence
» Memorization
» Ability to sustain attention
» Handwriting and fine motor skills

Several studies have demonstrated the negative impact of digital technology on recall of information in short-term memory, a crucial step in the learning process.[17]

It is easy to draw a straight line from the missing skills that classroom teachers are not seeing to the increase in screen use, both personal and learning.

In the prescient 2010 edition of his book, *The Shallows*, Nicholas Carr quoted the psychologist William James in describing how the brain creates neural pathways as it practices certain skills or content repeatedly.[18] James likened it to running water cutting through sand. As water continues to run, the channel that it previously cut is cut deeper and wider, so that eventually the water has no choice but to run through that path, unless something happens to make it change. Similarly, as students practice certain skills or don't practice certain skills, their brains are making pathways that become increasingly ingrained and increasingly difficult to avoid.

In the classroom, one can imagine this displaced learning in which certain skills that had been practiced and are still of value get neglected and forgotten. Carr quotes Norman Doidge, a research psychiatrist: "If we stop exercising our mental skills… we do not just forget them: the brain map space for those skills is turned over to the skills we practice instead."[19] The parts that are practiced become, to quote Carr, "the paths

---

Notes From The Field

Instead of giving three directions and off you go, I have to give one direction, repeat it back, off you go… and they come back to the carpet because they forgot. And I've never had to do that as much as I've been doing that the last couple of years.
First grade teacher
25 years experience

Now they all want to take shortcuts. They never want to write down… They abbreviate words that don't actually have an abbreviation. They leave words out… You can't even tell what they wrote.
5th grade teacher
19 years experience

We'll have an assessment with simple translation. They're given the word in Spanish and need to write in English. They spell the word so wrong in English that the computer can't recognize it and so they get it wrong. They're so used to autocorrect and the phone finishing words for them.
High school Spanish teacher
18 years experience

that most of us will take most of the time, and the farther we proceed down them, the more difficult it will become to turn back."[20]

Students don't need to remember verbal information if the neural pathway in their brain that gets a lot more repetition is the rewind button on their tablet or phone. Students don't need to develop fine motor skills or handwriting if they are swiping and tapping. Students don't need to practice that unnoticed skill of shifting and locking in focus from the whiteboard to the paper, back to white whiteboard, if they just stare at a single screen. Students don't need to memorize if they can just hit rewind or ask Google or ChatGPT. And without memorizing, knowing certain facts, names, dates, and relationships, it becomes more difficult to build the mental schema that serves as a foundation for new learning.

Reflective school leaders recognize that the rush to add ever more digital platforms moves classrooms and students further from the social, interactive, tactile learning experience that has been a hallmark of mainstream public schools. They recognize the need, with their leadership teams at both the district and school levels, to craft instructional visions that bring balance to what have become very fragmented learning experiences for many children.

Think back to what Rip Van Winkle saw, from the evolution in 2006 of classroom-based screens that students went to and used, but were not ubiquitous, to the much more extensive hardware of 2014 used to supplement but not supplant personal, intentional instruction by the teacher. What would Rip say about 2024?

What Rip Saw *

	2014	**2024**
Time spent interacting with the teacher and other students during learning	Most of the day	Varies, depending on length of time spent on passive individualized technology
Time spent by students using individualized learning platforms	15-30 minutes on average	Varies; up to 6 hours
Instructional Practices	• Reading aloud from physical books is commonplace, from kindergarten through high school • Students can follow multi-step directions • Handwriting and other fine motor skills are practiced	• Reading from screens, usually in isolation or, in primary grades, the book is read aloud by a digital narrator • Students struggle with holding more than one direction at a time in immediate working memory • Steep deterioration in handwriting, leading teachers to use Chromebooks to make writing legible, which results in further deterioration

*Based on classroom observations, teacher interviews, and data on technology usage in published research

TO WHAT END?

The move towards individualized screens and away from teachers and each other might be worth it if the results showed tremendous academic gains, but they do not. Whether the results are in math or reading, in social interactions or in a broad awareness about the world, in attention span or in ability to focus, the results are at best mixed, and for many groups of students, substantially worse.[21]

In reading, for example, the chapter on the collapse in the ability to sustain reading in Johann Hari's book should make every educator wonder about the efficacy of placing a screen as a reading teacher in front of young students. He quotes research that differentiates how the brain reads a book versus how we've trained it (or been trained) to read a screen. The way we skim and scan trains the brain to extract information, not necessarily to understand the text. A large set of studies cited in the chapter shows a "screen inferiority" when it comes to reading comprehension, with a gap equivalent to almost two-thirds of a year's growth for elementary school students within their first four, most formative years of learning how to read.[22]

Recent analysis of data from multiple sources, including the National Assessment of Educational Progress (NAEP), the Trends in International Mathematics and Science Study (TIMSS), and the Program for International Student Assessment (PISA), shows that the students for whom digital technology was heralded as a "leveling of the playing field" have actually had the steepest declines since 2015.[23]

Generally speaking, for the period of 2015 to 2025, while students at the highest achievement levels have remained relatively flat—increases on some assessments in some subject areas and modest declines on others—the lowest achieving students have had across-the-board declines.

Analysis of NAEP data from the 2024 assessment of 12th graders in math and reading shows a decline in scores from 2019 to 2024. This can be interpreted as pandemic-related learning loss. What the pandemic can't explain, however, is why scores were also lower in 2019 than they were in 2015. The percentage of students who scored "Below NAEP Basic" increased between 2015 and 2019 in both math and reading, a decline that appears to have started not with oft-cited struggles caused by COVID-19, but before that.[24]

With the benefit of hindsight, it is possible to look back and imagine several off-ramps where everyone from federal and state policy makers to school superintendents, principals, and other educational leaders might have pressed a pause button on the digital deluge. It is instructive, though, to consider this quote from a district-level leader who was a school principal in the mid-2010s.

> … "I was that principal who was the early technology adopter. We have to get tech in our classrooms. Everyone has a smart board of some kind, right? We have to start adopting it, using it, because it's there, right? It's not going to go away. How are you going to use Google to improve? And so, looking back in hindsight, I'm kind of like, oh….
>
> We did, after two years, start partnering the tech with collaborative conversations. We started partnering that with it; it's not just a word processing device, but how are you, for example, going on a virtual field trip? Those were the things we were trying to get them to do, where kids were working together to supplement their instruction, not have it be the instruction.
>
> Unfortunately, I think especially since COVID-19, it's really shifted into technology has become the instruction. And I'm not sure our teachers know how to go back. That's where we need to do better with refocusing them to use that technology as a support and not as the driver."

It is difficult to overstate how pervasive the sense was in 2012, 2014, 2016 that the future was now and anyone not on board was going to be left behind. But imagine if Rip had come from the future instead of the past, and told educators:

"I've seen a future where many districts take the status quo of 2014, and spend billions of dollars in hardware, software, programs, and connectivity. A screen is placed in front of every child, and students spend about half of their school day working in isolation. This screen time is piled onto the screen time they're already experiencing outside of school, and many students start to show signs of mental distress and dysregulated behavior. They disconnect from school, and absenteeism goes up, and enrollment drops because many parents figure their children can get an online education at home, so why send them to school? Teachers report drops in skills such as the ability to sustain reading or the desire to pay attention. Teaching takes more of a transactional quality than a transformational one, and classrooms get a lot quieter as less student talk takes place when the learning partner is a laptop, and students are wearing headphones. And as a payoff, our high-achieving students will be doing just about as well, but our lower-achieving students will be doing substantially worse in reading, writing, and math. Our students do get more tech-savvy, but it is difficult to assess whether the newfound skills are a result of what happens in school, or outside of it."

Would anyone accept that trade-off, with the benefit of hindsight? Or would they look for ways to walk back from it?

Will some school systems continue down the path of seeing individualized teaching platforms, learning in isolation, and now AI, as the panacea for academic shortcomings and achievement gaps? If so, a whole generation of learners is the subject of a mass experiment without a lot of research being done before its implementation. The kindergarten students of 2014 will graduate from high school in 2026. How prepared will they be for success in college, trade school, or the workplace after spending more than half of their schooling staring at screens, working on their own?

It is difficult to imagine school leaders who already see individualized instruction through screens as an optimal outcome being the ones who put up effective guardrails for the next panacea, artificial intelligence. Early research already shows that students who rely on AI not just to supplement and support their research and writing but to create, read, or summarize for them show lower retention of content, poorer writing skills, and less task persistence.[25]

How can school leaders navigate this next era of rapid change and encroaching technology? Will schools use artificial intelligence to enhance the learning experience without detracting from the human element? Or will moving from screen to screen become the norm, where kindergartners swipe rather than turn pages, and where high school students struggle with increased levels of isolation, anxiety, and fragmented focus?

WHAT WILL RIP SEE IN 2034? WILL THERE BE A COURSE CORRECTION?

Imagine a different future. Imagine a balanced school in 2034, which couples the best elements of analog era instruction with the benefits of digital era technology, that blends what was strong in 2014 with the infinite possibilities of technology in 2024.

Certainly, there were gaps in the classrooms that Rip saw in 2014 that could have been improved by thoughtful use of technology. Even with the best of intentions, instruction wasn't always standards-based, nor frequently research-based. Learning at times was a by-product, not the intended outcome of activities. Data, though widely available, wasn't always used efficiently. Large class sizes weren't made more manageable by effectively leveraging individualized platforms to allow the teacher more time for personalized small group instruction. It is easy to acknowledge that all was not well instructionally, while still knowing that something has been lost.

The classrooms that Rip saw in 2014 had a lot more student talk and collaboration. Teachers were more able to not just teach content, but mentor, guide, serve as role models, and inspire. Students practiced pre-content skills such as carrying information in their immediate working memory from the whiteboard to their paper and back. Placing items such as multiplication facts, important names and dates, and geographic, spatial relationships into short-term and then long-term memory was a daily occurrence, not a task outsourced to a search engine or AI.

Imagine the best of those classrooms augmented with technological components that, when added thoughtfully and with foresight, could make learning more engaging, visual, and authentic.

This 5th-grade teacher in a suburban district describes how she leverages technology when she is going to be out of the classroom on a planned absence. In her hands, technology is coupled strategically with the best that teachers bring.

> "When I know I have to be out of the classroom for an in-service, sometimes a review day is helpful; however, sometimes I don't have the luxury of skipping a math lesson on a substitute day. In order to stay caught up, I'll create a slideshow for the lesson, then record myself teaching it on Screencastify. I'll play the slideshow and do the examples on the screen using the Epic Pen app, and teach using a voice-over. Then, I'll load the lesson into Edpuzzle and put checking for understanding

questions into the guided practice section. This stops
the video and forces students to answer, giving them
immediate feedback, and me, immediate data. Edpuzzle
allows video restrictions, such as the inability to skip any
parts, which ensures the students watch the whole thing.
I'll provide students with their independent practice
assignment instructions at the very end of the video,
and if I'm available, I can use Go Guardian to monitor
their lesson progress and answer questions via chat, if
needed. This makes it possible for me to teach the lesson
in a way that is familiar to students, get feedback from
Edpuzzle to gauge their understanding, and not lose an
instructional day due to an unavoidable absence."

Reflective public-school leaders understand the need for a
balanced blend of traditional, personal, intentional instruction
and learning with technological innovation. Rather than holding
two conflicting versions of education in which one displaces the
other simply because it is more modern, balanced public schools
are places that allow students to engage with their peers and
use technology to enhance learning and build connections. It
is possible to imagine schools as dynamic places of learning by
taking an "and" approach rather than an "either/or" one. Schools
can be places where students navigate not just content, but also
social interactions and citizenship, AND schools can be places
where technology steps in to augment student learning through
individualized re-teaching, in-the-moment diagnostics, data
analysis, and AI support.

In these balanced schools, strategic school leaders realize
that adopting new technological advancements and platforms
without a clearly defined instructional vision and strategic
decision-making can lead to haphazard implementation,
disconnected initiatives, and, at times, conflicting agendas.
School leaders in these balanced schools of 2034 have developed
not just a process for adopting technology—which most districts
already had in place in 2014—but also a filter for keeping
unnecessary technology out. They also have a systematic plan
for the implementation of initiatives that prioritize student
learning rather than the use of the technology itself. Chasing the
next innovation without having carefully considered its impact,
without having determined what it was displacing, without

having sufficiently trained staff, or without putting in place implementation guardrails, it does not happen in these schools. These school leaders realize that the six-hour day of 2034 is no longer than the six-hour day of 2014, and that continuing to add platforms or AI just because the district next door rushed into it results in a scattered, fragmented instructional program, which does not maximize learning time, the one resource that cannot be replaced.

WHERE NOW?

The following steps are challenging but vital. Classrooms—and decision-making about classrooms—in America need an overhaul from where we find ourselves a quarter of the way into the 21st century. The response cannot be to blindly add more technology as AI becomes more ingrained and software companies dictate the daily schedule to school leaders.

The post-pandemic landscape in schools has lacked clarity. One researcher described it as "Our education system is struggling in its entirety. The bounce-back we envisioned—a fiery national mobilization to overcome learning setbacks—has eluded us... No group, from students to parents to teachers to administrators, feels the same connection to our schools that they once did."[26]

We think school and district-level leaders need to strategically and thoughtfully commit to and coordinate the implementation of the following critical processes in mainstream public schools:

1. The development of an instructional vision for a student experience that strikes a careful balance between the incredible opportunities presented by evolving technology and the interaction, modeling, and personal connections that have been a hallmark of mainstream public schools. A clear and cohesive instructional vision—not to be confused with the broader, gauzy "Mission statement" of school board documents and website banners—aligns initiatives and expenditures with the district's core values and beliefs.

2. A re-grounding in human, intentional instruction based on established research about how the brain learns best, including the development of a common language of instruction, that has long been a crucial component in high-performing schools and districts. A systemic challenge mentioned by teachers we interviewed was that decision-making following the pandemic eschewed balanced, human-centered, intentional instruction for isolating individualized platforms, often while promoting these programs as more "student-centered."

These isolating options missed the pandemic's lessons about schools: in theory, students were receiving the necessary content. In reality, the content is only a part of the school equation. The interaction with caring adults and other students is as much a part of the educational experience as the content. No laptop is going to be able to inspire high school students to care about Shakespeare, government, or the environment. And no laptop is going to be able to jump rope during recess, teach students how to navigate rules around handball, or listen to or make a story come alive during read-aloud in the same way that a teacher can.

3. The purposeful use of new and existing technology to supplement, rather than supplant, instruction, coupled with a technology filter that prompts decision makers at every level of school systems to consider the following questions as a starting point:

> **a.** What does this technology displace?
> **b.** Will the results of this technology be substantially better to offset the opportunity cost of the lost social interaction?

4. The re-emphasizing of communication and durable skills that students need as well-rounded members of society, as well as a re-examination of displaced learning skills that students are no longer practicing sufficiently, with detrimental impacts.

Several surveys of American corporations reveal the traits and characteristics that employers are looking for, and are finding lacking, in recent graduates from both high school and college.[27] As AI continues to shape how we obtain, use, and process information, schools must provide students with the development of language and durable skills. Tools such as critical thinking, communication, and adaptability will become increasingly essential as technology continues to rapidly advance. Technology threatens to take over functions of the brain that humans have developed over time, such as short-term memorization, learning how to navigate a map, communicating both verbally and in writing, determining if information is valid and reliable, and relating to other humans.

The integration of specific and strategic language and collaboration skills into a common instructional framework will allow students the opportunity to practice and reinforce the critical ability to engage in deep, rigorous, high-level thinking and partnership with others.

5. An adaptive sustainability plan that takes a whole community approach. A critical and often neglected part of systemic change is the sustainability plan. The lack of such a plan is often also the reason for change to fail, and for the pendulum to swing in a reactionary spasm in the other direction. Finding the right balance in 2034 means partnering with outside entities that also contribute to students' well-being, and not doing so will make the task for schools infinitely harder. Students don't check their overloaded outside brain at the door as they enter school and then reclaim it when they leave. They travel with the same brain for 24 hours, and that brain is constantly bombarded with digital information and distractions, both inside of school and out. Only focusing on what happens inside the school walls will not be as successful as taking a more expansive, realistic view of the lives our students lead outside of school.

It cannot be overstated that the change that schools will need to implement to find the right balance in 2034 might be among the toughest tasks school leaders face. These challenges are on par with dealing with a pandemic, closing the achievement gap, and dealing with mental health crises. It is so difficult because it envelops all these previous challenges, and many more. School leaders face teacher and administrator shortages, public doubts about mainstream public schools, and a departure into alternative forms of K-12 education. School leaders are challenged by dysregulated student behavior, increased absenteeism, and societal schisms that make education a partisan tug of war. All of this is happening in the face of the pervasive sense that technology is speeding up faster than the system can assimilate it, and that students and districts may be left behind.

It will take courageous leadership at every level—classroom, school building, district office—to not rush into adoption.

Frankly, it is easier to let the digital curriculum vendors convince school leaders that the solution is putting the students on one platform for 2 hours daily for English Language Arts, and another for 90 minutes of math, along with a third option for interactive science or social studies.

Throw in some YouTube activities for physical education, and students can spend a whole day without ever picking up a pencil or interacting with each other. But at what cost?

School leaders will need to keep their instructional vision at the forefront at all times. They must stay grounded in their shared values in order to balance using the tools of the day with the durable skills that allow students to connect.

And the school day is not enough. It is critical to remember that while this book deals mostly with the impacts of classroom-based technology on students and their development, students are enveloped in technology in the many hours outside of school. The calendar year has 8760 hours. Students only spend about 1080 in school. A whole community approach that helps students find a healthy balance with their digital technology must include parent education to teach parents about the dangers of a screen-based childhood, as well as articulation with after-school and summer programs, pre-school providers, and possibly health care systems.

The decisions made by leaders about how students spend their day will impact generations of learners. Will students spend an ever-increasing amount of time on individualized screens and instructional panaceas promised by software companies? Or will districts take a balanced approach, leveraging technology but not delegating their most critical function—teaching and learning—to algorithms?

It is a future with two distinct paths.

Down one path, we see a present and a future where adults' reading habits continue to decline, are not well-informed, selectively pursue information that meets their pre-existing viewpoint, and struggle to connect with others.[28] It is a present and a future where young adults spend upwards of nine hours per day on screens, and more than three hours per day on social media, and have inverted the happiness curve, going from being among the happiest age groups to the most depressed. It is a present and a future where children struggle to sustain focus, show more dysregulated behavior, have trouble recalling facts from long-term memory, and hold information in immediate working memory.

That path leads to continued high levels of disconnectedness, behavioral challenges, chronic absenteeism, academic and social gaps, and continued mental health crises.

The other leads to the development of a balanced instructional vision with intentional instruction that fosters personal connections and focuses on developing language and durable skills.

It isn't difficult to envision that some districts will take the easier path, especially in difficult-to-staff districts where teachers are scarce and software promises to meet every student where they are academically.

It is more difficult to take the second approach and do the hard work of arriving at a shared vision, of investing in the human capital rather than the hardware, of professional development, of arguments and disagreements, especially in the face of

persistent criticism, short-sighted political goals and a public
that has come to see school buildings as an option, rather than
the norm.

THE SECOND PATH

The answers are out there. Not every district has fallen prey to
the empty promises of quick and pain-free hardware-based
solutions. Some districts and leaders are showing the way, if only
others will follow.

Excerpts from interviews with two school leaders pursuing the
second path conclude this chapter. One leader, a superintendent
of a large exurban school district with more than two dozen
schools, was previously the chief technology officer of her
school district, has held state-level leadership positions in
technology-based organizations, and was awarded Technology
Administrator of the Year in 2019 by her state's school
administrator association.

The second leader is currently the Director of Technology in
her medium-sized suburban school district of thirteen schools.
Her district has bucked the trend of declining achievement
levels described earlier, with its student achievement levels
significantly higher than pre-pandemic levels.

It is important to note that both educators are technology
advocates and that neither one has rose colored glasses
about technology use. Look for the recurring themes in their
comments.

First, the superintendent...

On phones in the classrooms and on training students:

> "If you put hard, firm rules, 'we're going to block this' or
> whatever, kids will just find a way around it. You're just
> encouraging them to bypass the system we set up, so they get
> burner phones, they get fake phones. They put that phone
> in the pouch so you see them put a phone in the pouch, but

they have another phone in their backpack. You know, it's better just to train them to use it appropriately... We'd rather teach students to be responsible."

On teacher professional development:

"... We stopped a few years ago doing technology trainings separate from curriculum trainings, because we don't want technology to be used just for the sake of technology. We want it to be used in a way that really enhances the instructional design, because we feel like kids are already on screens too much. And we believe in utilizing technology in the classroom, and that there are benefits for students when we utilize technology, but only if we do it in an intentional way. Otherwise, we're just adding to that already exorbitant amount of screen time that kids have. Because you see it, you go out to restaurants, kids are sitting there on their screens, they're in their cars, they're on... it's a babysitter tool a lot these days. So, we don't want to just say, you know, we're going to take the opposite extreme, we're not going to use any screens, but we want to be really intentional with it. So, we embed it into our technology training and our curriculum training.

We're modeling for teachers: 'Here's where and when and how you could utilize technology, where it really pushes the needle on student achievement, as opposed to just using it because it's cool and using technology for the sake of using technology.'"

On Artificial Intelligence:

"Our entire approach around AI is that it has to be human-centered, that you have to prompt the human before you prompt AI, and that AI's purpose is to magnify our own intelligence; we should never use it as a replacement. It's not a replacement. I think the very core and essence of what we do in education is relational-based. We know that part of what really impacts student achievement and the student experience is the relevance of what they're learning, not just the rigor of it, but the relevance. And part of that relevance is relational. And you can't have a computer do that."

On individualized platforms:

"We did that on purpose to fill those gaps coming out of COVID-19, and so that is the only screen time that we ever said 'Kids need to use it X amount of minutes per day', but as we were rolling that out, we polled what schools were utilizing, and spoke with principals and said, 'Okay, we're going to move to using this platform. You have to get rid of this other program, because you can't have kids on screens all day long. You're not going to double (up)- you're getting rid of the other one, because if we are going to have kids on screens, they're going to be on screens for this.' So we really intentionally made sure we talked to people about getting rid of those comparable programs because you could see people buying into 'oh, if this one's good, and I'm going to get this much bang, and this one's good, and I'm going to get that much bang, why not do both?' Well, why not do both? Because then you have kids on screens all day long."

On working with the community and developing durable skills:

"Like other districts, we developed a portrait of a graduate. But I really don't like just hanging posters on the wall for the sake of having a poster hanging on the wall. So we've spent the last couple of years really pushing those identified competencies out into the community. What does it look like in the classroom? And how are we actually ensuring that we're developing these competencies, ensuring that our students have a lot of opportunity to talk, a lot of opportunity to work on real-world problems, and collaborate, and exercise those critical thinking skills... We do our cabinet walkthroughs, and the principal comes with us, and we stop after every classroom, and we analyze, 'okay, we were in there for X amount of time, how many times could they have done a turn and talk? How many times could they have given students a little bit more time, or given students a chance to learn from their mistakes?

We really do have a transformation in education. Because the (displaced) skills are vital, and they're important, but there are also very outdated things that we have kids doing that aren't necessary. We haven't found what is necessary that maybe replaces that.... That transformation has to take place or... we really are going to become obsolete..."

Next, the Director of Technology...

On the technology adoption process in her district in the mid-2010s:

"We didn't have a lot of money, which kind of worked to our advantage in terms of we weren't buying everything. I mean, we bought a set of iPods before there were iPads, and that was with a grant that I wrote- a large grant at the time of $250,000.

I think the first systematic thing that we did was in 2015 or 16, we started using a program for reading intervention. To do that, we had to get Chromebooks, and the IT department didn't want to do anything that wasn't Windows-based, so there were these natural slowdown points. We eventually found a workaround, but it wasn't fast. Probably took two years.

We really got going when the state assessment went digital, and we had to do it quickly. But even then, there was a lot of discussion before we did anything. We had a technology needs assessment committee, made up of administrators, teachers, and community members. And we had a group of teachers called BETA, who were the ones piloting innovative tech. Our Assistant Superintendent was great about letting us try different things, discuss, so that by the time we made a decision, we were good about what we were going to chase."

On teacher professional development:

"The first things we implemented were quick but with small groups of teachers, and thank goodness, because it really helped us see what we needed to work on, what training teachers needed. You would think it's the same, but it isn't. The classroom management, for example, is different."

On process for assessing opportunity cost:

"It really helped us, I think, to not have a lot of money at the time, so we had to be really strategic. When we considered a program, the first conversation was 'you're giving up instructional time, so it'd better be worth it.' Time and money- we didn't have a lot of either- so we had to be smart about it."

On the common language of instruction, COVID-19 and the aftermath:

"I don't think we could have done it without a common language of instruction. Our journey was slow and steady, but thank goodness we had done the work on instruction first. Having a common language has stuck, and our academic program has never been stronger. The work (on a common language) made the COVID-19 shutdowns plausible. When it was over, and we stabilized after a year or two, we had teachers who wanted to get back to teaching. I was kind of glad when the ESSER (Elementary and Secondary School Emergency Relief) funds went away. It made us prioritize again. For a while there, you were just getting stuff thrown at you, and you couldn't say no. ESSER going away made us go back to 'what do we value the highest?' and it was direct instruction, the structure of how we do things. There's a consistency there, and if it doesn't fit, we don't do it. We have a lot of autonomy at the teacher level, but you have to have shared values, or it doesn't work."

Conclusion

The reader doesn't need to look hard to find the recurring themes between these two leaders, and one has to look very hard to find a hint of thinking about technology as the panacea.

Instead, what one largely sees is the commitment and belief in humans, in training and discussing, and reasoning. And one also sees the throughline of what matters:

» Intentional training: students, teachers, principals
» Communication at the adult level to determine values and priorities and assess opportunity costs
» Strategic, purposeful implementation
» A common language of instruction as the framework and the filter for what gets adopted

The second path is more difficult than the first.

There are no silver bullets just hard work, purposeful instruction, and a common vision of what instruction is supposed to look like.

Chapter 2
Instructional Vision

"In the long run, men only hit what they aim for."

Henry David Thoreau (1817 - 1862)
American Author, Poet, and Philosopher

To find the right balance between the implementation of technology and human connection, districts must start with an Instructional Vision. The Instructional Vision is the decision-making roadmap for the most critical decisions made about teaching and learning. It answers the question, "How does the district do business?" and serves as the primary tool for instructional decision-making. It is as much a tool for deciding what and how to teach as it is for understanding what to exclude or abandon.

DuFour and Marzano[1] emphasize that effective instructional leadership requires a clear and shared vision of learning that guides coherent action across classrooms, schools, and systems. Similarly, Yukl[2] identifies the articulation of vision and direction-setting as a core leadership function necessary for aligning organizational practices and sustaining improvement.

Districts that wish to actively shape the instructional landscape of future schools must develop and follow a carefully crafted Instructional Vision. Without this roadmap, the outcomes in 2034 and beyond may be far from the goal of well-rounded students prepared to address the human and technical challenges facing humanity. The instructional program that students experience is the living embodiment of an Instructional Vision.

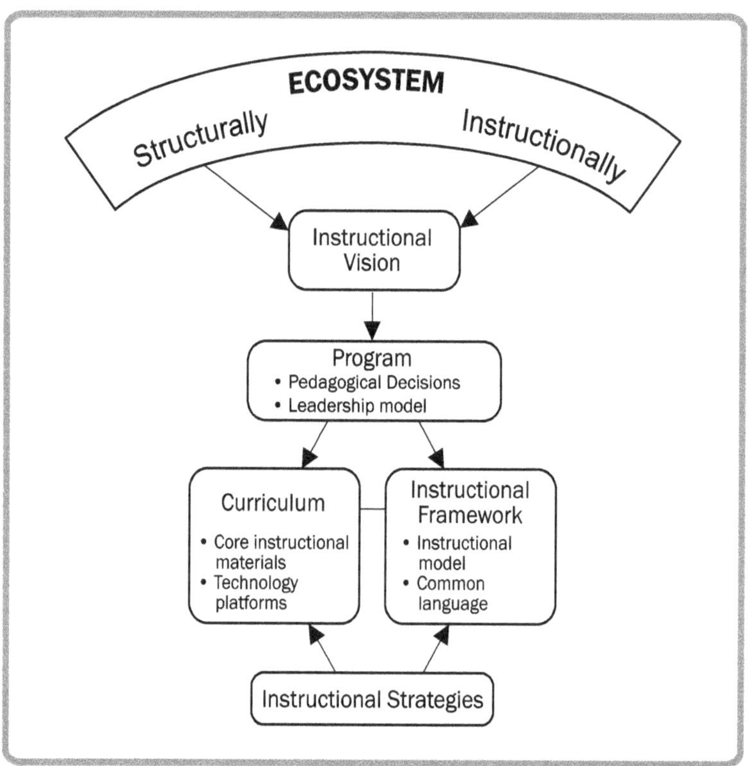

Developing an effective Instructional Vision is the culmination of a series of deliberate data-driven decisions that school communities make:

» Determining the instructional model and agreeing on a common language
» Pondering questions about leadership, training, and development
» Allocating resources
» Carefully considering curriculum adoption and abandonment

In today's technological age, where screen time is pervasive for children, educational teams should consider how much human and non-human contact students have in a school day. This consideration, and ultimate decision-making, is critical to the development of a district's Instructional Vision.

Combining or collapsing, adopting or abandoning, promoting
or demoting programs or practices without an Instructional
Vision often results in a lot of change but no clear direction.
Each decision is independent of the next, resulting in a
lack of commitment to the changes and a general sense of
disconnectedness.

So, how does a district develop an Instructional Vision? A lot of
little steps and three big ones:

1. Identifying, communicating, and implementing a
   collaborative leadership model
2. Identifying and giving voice to the district's core
   values around which an Instructional Vision will be
   built
3. Communicating broad but measurable goals and
   objectives

In education, a clearly articulated Instructional Vision is more
than just a formality; it is the guiding compass for teaching
and learning. The district's Instructional Vision drives the
development of an instructional program and allows educational
teams to develop a common instructional framework. For the
Instructional Vision to be an effective tool for progress, it must
be a living document, used regularly to guide teaching and
learning, and updated annually or when data indicates changes
are necessary. The power of a compelling Instructional Vision is
that it gives every member of the district or school community
a common schema for decision-making and contributing to the
work they do together.

1. Identifying, communicating, and implementing a collaborative leadership model

There are many models of leadership, and strong leaders
understand how to apply the right leadership style to the
situation at hand.

Style of Leadership	Strength of Style	Weakness of Style
Hierarchical/ Autocratic[3][4]	Leaders are identified through an organizational chart, and everyone knows who is in charge. This style is needed in emergencies.	Decisions may not include a broad understanding of the situation or consider other perspectives. In an educational setting, this style may not be focused on teaching and learning.
Instructional[5][6]	Leadership is role-based (principal, assistant principal, instructional coach) with an emphasis on setting a clear instructional vision, observing classrooms and providing feedback and aligning curriculum, assessment, and standards, and using data to improve instruction. Authority typically flows top-down.	It can overload administrators as they are the key leaders of the work, and it can limit teacher agency. Sustainability depends on a few individuals.
Distributed[7][8]	Leaders involve team members in the decision-making process. This style fosters collaboration and encourages a wide range of perspectives. In an educational setting, this style is focused on teaching and learning. Does not forsake hierarchical responsibilities.	Decisions often take longer. This style is not effective for emergencies.

In practice, hierarchical leadership concentrates authority and decision-making at the top of the organizational chart. Identified leaders are the decision makers, and in-line staff follow the directives from above. Hierarchical leaders are often highly capable, charismatic, intelligent individuals who lead from a single vantage point. A strength of this style of leadership is that it is clear who is in charge, and everyone knows who to take direction from.

As Northouse explains, "Leadership is a process whereby an individual influences a group of individuals to achieve a common goal," a definition that aligns closely with hierarchical structures in which influence is exercised primarily through positional authority.[9]

However, as problems become more complex, it is difficult for a single leader to have all the knowledge and skills to effectively lead and bring about meaningful change. Where a hierarchical approach to leadership focuses on getting business done in a top-down manner, Instructional leadership focuses the work on teaching and learning. In this model, the responsibility rests almost entirely with formal leaders (principal, assistant principal, etc.) and does not harness the power of the team.

Distributed Leadership is a system of practice composed of a collection of interacting components: leaders, followers, and situations. It views leadership as both a structure and a practice, extending beyond positional authority. Although Distributed Leadership involves multiple leaders with distinct interrelated responsibilities, it is not shared leadership where groups make all the decisions. In Distributed Leadership, formal leaders set clear guardrails defining the focus of the work, expectations, and timelines while empowering teams to determine how the work is implemented.[11][12]

In this way, Distributed Leadership is a system that assembles the strengths of multiple individuals, including those directly engaged in teaching, to make well-informed decisions encompassing many perspectives and knowledge bases.[13]

Distributed Leadership is aimed at moving leadership out of the hierarchical offices (district administrators and principals) and into schools and classrooms. However, hierarchical leaders are not absolved of their formal responsibilities to lead. For example, they still implement state law and district policies. They still review data, needs assessments, and any other relevant material and bring it to the attention of the various leadership teams. They are still responsible for their staff and student outcomes. To ensure that Distributed Leadership can flourish, leaders should build support across the system by focusing on strengths and progress. They review core values and set the expectation of open conversation and mutual respect. They model listening to various points of view and new ideas, and the process for reaching consensus. They ensure that the district and schools operate effectively *and* keep the focus on teaching and learning.

The advantages of Distributed Leadership are:

» Harnesses the collective human capital
» Compensates for individual weaknesses
» Improves communication and cooperation
» Sets a higher level of commitment for agreed-upon decisions
» Allows for diverse perspectives and, therefore, includes a focus on the needs of all groups of students
» Spurs innovation
» Encompasses higher learning
» Improves job satisfaction through opportunities for individuals to influence decisions that affect their work
» Improves employee retention
» Increases motivation and optimism for all employees

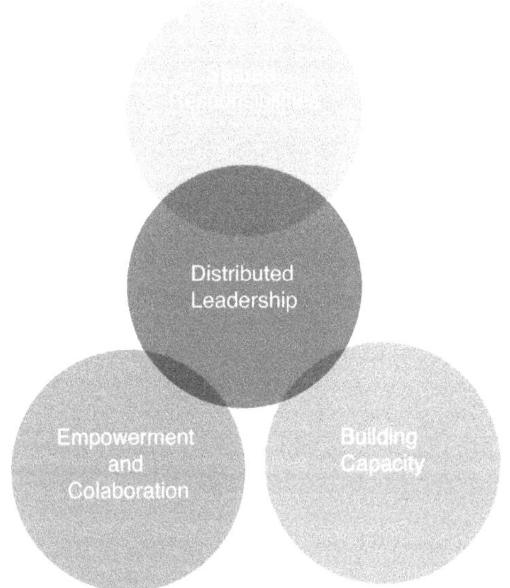

The Key Aspects of This Model include:

Shared Responsibilities: Rather than relying on a single person or a small leadership team, different members of the school community take on leadership roles.

Empowerment and Collaboration: All members of the school community are encouraged to lead initiatives and contribute to school improvement efforts. This collaboration can lead to more comprehensive solutions and a stronger sense of ownership.

Building Capacity: By distributing leadership, school systems can build a wider pool of capable leaders who are prepared to take on more significant roles over time, creating a more sustainable leadership structure.

To establish a Distributed Leadership framework in a district, the Superintendent and Assistant Superintendents must first establish the parameters for the composition of an Instructional Leadership Team (ILT) or Professional Learning Communities (PLCs).

We recommend that each school site select members, ensuring that each grade level and/or content area and specialty (e.g., special education) has a representative member on their school ILT. The collective School ILTs make up the District ILT. The District ILT members will be the guiding coalition for developing the Instructional Vision for the entire district. Based on the needs of the district, the ILT may develop additional committees such as a Culture and Climate Team, an English Learner Team, a Behavior Team, and a Special Education Team.

This ensures high-quality decision-making during the development and implementation of the Instructional Vision. For example, the chart below represents how a three-school district ILT structure might look:

Composition of District ILT		
School #1 Elementary Site ILT	School # 2 Middle School Site ILT	School # 3 High School Site ILT
Team Members: • Principal • Special Education Teacher • 1 teacher per grade level • Counselor • English Learner Teacher	Team Members: • Principal • Assistant Principal • 1 teacher per subject area • 1 Elective Teacher • Counselor • English Learner Teacher • Special Education Teacher	Team Members: • Principal • Assistant Principal • 1 teacher per subject area • 1 Elective Teacher • Counselor • English Learner Teacher • Special Education Teacher

The Work of the Instructional Leadership Teams

Instructional Leadership Teams (ILTs) are foundational to the success of a district or school. ILT members bring others along, opening dialogue, collaboration, and strategic planning. The ILT plans for the instructional program, the role of technology, the social-emotional needs of students, and the development of durable skills as foundational components of the district's Instructional Vision.

An example of an important question that a District ILT team should consider is how the use of individualized screen instruction evolves across the grade levels. In our district, how much time should a kindergarten student be interacting with adults and peers versus a screen, and how does that look different in grade 5? In grade 9?

Typical tasks of a District ILT will include data analysis, developing a common language of instruction, goal development, establishing clear success criteria, planning for professional learning, and delivering professional learning aligned to the Instructional Vision.

Each Site ILT takes the work of the District ILT back to their school staff.

They conduct Site ILT meetings to plan next steps for their school based on their student data and input from all educational staff members. They set goals and timelines, and provide professional learning to their colleagues during staff meetings. They also schedule collaborative planning days and peer observation or professional development days. In this way, the Site ILT mirrors the work of the District ILT but adapts the work to meet the specific needs of their staff and students.

Distributed Leadership is essential to the effective functioning of ILTs and must be the solid foundation for the work. If leaders are using Distributive Leadership as a ruse for top-down directives, team members will quickly become disillusioned with the process and detach from the team. Or worse yet, become saboteurs. As Yukl cautions, "Empowerment is not just the delegation of responsibility, but the sharing of power and influence," underscoring that distributed leadership must be genuine rather than symbolic.[14]

Additionally, the work of the ILT is a commitment to excellence in education and requires a significant commitment of time. Bloomberg and Pitchford emphasize the importance of collective efficacy, stating that "when educators believe together that they can positively impact student learning, the results are exponential."[15] Leaders who do not create and stick to a well-developed scope and sequence for meetings and professional learning will quickly see the ILT lose coherence and effectiveness.

Important Hallmarks of Distributed Leadership

Several key characteristics define successful teams, offering valuable insights into how they can foster better teaching outcomes and student success.

One fundamental characteristic of effective ILTs is clear, shared goals. ILTs that establish and maintain a common vision are significantly more successful in their collaborative efforts. When educators align on objectives—whether it's enhancing instructional practices, improving student engagement, or discussing the use of technology —they are better equipped to coordinate their efforts and support each other. This alignment fosters a sense of purpose and direction, which is crucial for collective motivation and achievement.

As Goddard, Goddard, and Tschannen-Moran observe, "Teacher collaboration is positively related to student achievement when it is focused on student learning and instructional improvement", highlighting the critical role of shared goals and coordinated efforts in effective teams.[16]

Another essential characteristic is open and effective communication. ILTs that prioritize this are more adept at addressing challenges, sharing resources, and refining their practices based on collaborative input. Effective communication involves not only the exchange of information but also active listening and constructive feedback.

ILTs with diverse skill sets and perspectives perform better when their unique viewpoints, innovative thinking, problem-solving, and perspectives are encouraged. This diversity enhances creativity and allows teams to tackle a broader range of challenges. Transparent and respectful dialogue among team members is a crucial element for high-functioning teams.

Effective teams in educational settings exhibit a strong sense of trust and mutual respect. Trust among team members is vital for creating a supportive and collaborative environment. When educators trust each other, they are more willing to take risks, share new ideas, and support one another through challenges. As Lencioni asserts, "Trust is the foundation of real teamwork," highlighting its essential role in fostering collaboration and collective responsibility.[17] This trust nurtures a positive team culture, which is instrumental in achieving educational goals and fostering professional growth. To build trust and respect, leaders must ensure they follow through on their promises and hold everyone accountable for their actions. Good work must be recognized publicly, and dissent must be addressed swiftly, albeit privately.

How Do Leaders Foster Meaningful Collaboration?

Model, model, model!

Distributive Leaders who provide clear direction, support team members, demonstrate follow-through, and facilitate collaboration contribute significantly to a team's performance. They recognize and leverage the strengths of individual team members. Creating an environment where everyone can thrive includes the development and emphasis on shared core values. Leadership is crucial in modeling the core values as the blueprint for how team members interact with one another.

Through this intentional Distributed Leadership, educational organizations can build teams that not only enhance their own effectiveness but also contribute significantly to the success and well-being of their students. When collaborative teams falter, it is often because they do not have clearly defined core values to anchor interactions, discussions, and decisions.

2. Identifying and giving voice to the district's core values around which a vision will be built

Importance of Core Values			
Set a Strong Foundation	Provide a Clear Framework for Making Decisions	Ensure Consistency and Fairness	Foster a Positive and Inclusive Culture

Core values are the fundamental beliefs, agreements, and guiding principles that shape an organization's culture, decision-making processes, and actions. Lencioni tells us, "core values define what an organization stands for and guide its decision-making, culture, and behavior.[18] Without them, an organization risks inconsistency, confusion, and disengagement." For all members of the organization, core values serve as the compass that directs all efforts toward a shared vision. These values are not just abstract ideals. They influence every aspect of the educational environment, from interactions with students and staff to policy development, human resources practices, budgeting decisions, curriculum and technology adoption and abandonment, and community engagement.

Teamwork, respect, integrity, innovation, kindness, collaboration, patience, knowledge, trust, dignity, etc., are all examples of core values. The list of core values is infinite, and effective teams take time to explore which ones apply most to their work together.

Discovering the ILT's Core Values

Each of us has a set of values that guide the choices we make in life. A person who values collaboration will seek the group's input before making decisions. A person who values respect will reflect it in the way they talk to people, how they listen to them, and how they see individuals as worth their time and energy.

Personally, we could each list many values that inform how we live. When an ILT first forms, knowing what the group collectively values allows them to navigate the work in a professional, efficient, and effective manner. The group's values become a common platform, an agreement that shapes the culture of the ILT.

Teams will likely struggle with the growing intrusion of technology on the development of strong social connections and the resulting impact on relationships, communication, and social interactions. The impact of technology on the educational environment must be at the forefront of the team's minds when they discuss core values. They must consider how technology is impacting the well-being of staff and students and how or if their values regarding technology contribute to their decision-making.

For example, if the team values clear communication, do they have guidelines for texting, email, phones, and in-person discussions? Is it okay to contact parents via text to discuss a disciplinary situation? When is texting or email acceptable, and when should staff use a phone call or an in-person meeting? Does a virtual meeting count as in-person? The layers of discussion are complex, which is why leaders must dedicate time to the process of identifying core values and clearly articulating how the values will show up in the day-to-day business of schools.

The wise facilitator ensures that all voices are heard and understood and does not rush the core value development process. In an ILT where the core values have been jointly developed by team members from all levels and reflect a deeply held consensus of what is most important, the core values provide a template for how we do our work and relate to each other. By clearly defining and actively implementing core values, ILTs ensure their decision-making and initiatives align with what they value. They guide the ILT in creating positive, equitable, and effective learning environments for students and adults, ultimately leading to better student outcomes and a stronger, more cohesive school community.

ILTs that have not taken the time to establish their core values have lost an opportunity to define who they are and how they will work together, which may create unnecessary conflict and disharmony when consequential decisions need to be made.

Values are not static ideals but dynamic principles that evolve with the organization, helping to navigate challenges and seize opportunities while staying true to the organization's deeply held beliefs .[19] They are a filter for decision-making; therefore, an ILT can quickly lose its way if the values they created are not regularly reviewed. Without reviewing core values, a team may run the risk of making decisions that do not align with the values of the team or that are not in the best interest of students.

3. Communicating broad but measurable goals and objectives

The Instructional Vision is a comprehensive document that lays out the road map for where the organization wants to go, providing specific annual goals and actions that build toward the vision. It includes the theory of action taken by the organization. A theory of action explains the basis for decisions in an if/then format. The Instructional Vision also identifies the responsibilities of all staff members and the metrics of success.

Providing supporting information that is targeted toward the specifics of the plan, including a sample Model School Day, the annual Professional Development Plan, and the Technology Filter, increases clarity for the implementation of the plan.

What should be included in an Instructional Vision Document?

Outline of an Instructional Vision

• Instructional Vision Statement
  • Instructional Program
    • Instructional Framework
    • Curriculum
    • Annual Goals
      • Year 1 Goals
      • Year 2 Goals
      • Year 3 Goals
      • Year 4 Goals
      • Year 5 Goals

• Theory of Action
• Responsibilities and Actions by Role
• Metrics for Success and Ongoing Evaluation of Goals

• Supporting Information
  • Model School Day (one each for specific grade spans: TK -Kindergarten, Primary Elementary, Upper Elementary, Middle School, High School)
  • Annual Professional Learning Plan
  • Technology Filter

Instructional Vision Statement

To develop a relevant Instructional Vision statement, teams should engage in deep data dives that include both quantitative and qualitative indicators to identify the strengths and gaps in teaching and learning. Once these have been identified, the team can leverage research-based pedagogies, aligned with their values, that have the greatest likelihood to build on the strengths, close gaps in skills or knowledge, and positively impact outcomes.

An Instructional Vision statement should identify the instructional needs and state how the needs will be addressed.

For example, an Instructional Vision statement could be:

> "In Schools Next School District, we recognize that the educational ecosphere is impacted by the overwhelming influence of technology, with detrimental effects on

students' learning outcomes, durable skills development, and mental health. In SNSD, we will thoughtfully balance personal, intentional instruction with the use of technology tools, which will foster a healthy learning environment that supports children's overall cognitive, language, and social-emotional development."

As a team's values drive the Instructional Vision statement, the Instructional Vision statement sets the stage for the development of the Instructional Program.

The Instructional Program defines the entire school year. Whereas the Instructional Vision answers the questions "what are our needs and how should we address them?" The Instructional Program answers the question "how exactly will the school operationalize the Instructional Vision?" When thinking about the Instructional Program, it is helpful to consider both the Instructional Framework and the Curriculum.

Instructional Framework

The Instructional Framework includes specific pedagogical decisions for teaching and learning. What lesson structure will we use, when, and why? How do we talk about teaching and learning? What common language of instruction have we agreed upon? What types of activities will we implement and for what learning purposes? The Instructional Framework delineates what approaches to teaching and learning the district will be focusing on to reach the intended outcomes.

Examples include:

» Gradual Release of Responsibility
» Guided Inquiry
» Problem-Based Learning
» Intentional Discourse, etc.

Part of the district's framework should incorporate the appropriate use of technology. This instructional framework drives the plan for instructional improvements and thus drives the Professional Learning Plan.

The Curriculum

The Curriculum includes the materials used, including text, technological platforms, common assessments, master schedules for secondary schools, and model day schedules for elementary campuses. Each curricular decision should be clearly aligned with the Instructional Vision.

Annual Goals

For schools to make progress toward their Instructional Vision, team members should develop instructional goals highlighting how they want the district/school to look in 3 - 5 years. Then they should identify the most impactful actions that will be taken each successive year.

For example, based on the Instructional Vision above, a Year One Goal might be:

> Instructional Leadership Team (ILT) members will strengthen their capacity to improve teaching and learning. They will accomplish this by improving their pedagogical knowledge and skills and focusing on standards-aligned intentional instruction. They will foster a healthy environment by abandoning misaligned technology and practices and will focus on the development of durable skills at all grade levels.

Deciding on an Instructional Program results from a comprehensive data analysis and should be done in tandem with the development of the Instructional Vision. The selection of the Instructional Program is a critical component for the development of the Instructional Vision. It is important to allocate sufficient time and resources to this process and the ultimate decision. All relevant educational partners (district administrators, principals, teachers, classified staff, community partners, and students) should be included. Communication and collaboration are key to selecting the most advantageous Instructional Program.

This process should not be rushed.

District leadership should plan for multiple planning meetings in the summer preceding the launch of the Instructional Vision. Here is a sample of how a district might structure the meetings to complete the work:

Planning Team - Sample Agendas

Meeting #1 8:00 a.m. - 2:00 p.m. Agenda:	Meeting #2 8:00 a.m. - 2:00 p.m. Agenda:	Meeting #3 8:00 a.m. - 2:00 p.m. Agenda:
• Welcome • Overview of the Instructional Leadership Team program • Analyze Relevant Data to determine key challenges and barriers to higher student achievement • Ascertain District's Core Values	• Welcome • Review of Data Analysis from meeting #1 • Finalize District's Core Values • Write Educational Vision Statement • Determine the Instructional Framework	• Welcome • Review Educational Vision Statement and Instructional Framework from Meeting #2 • Develop the Annual Goals (years 1– 5) • Develop the Criteria for Success (metrics) • Develop Responsibilities and Actions by Role

Theory of Action

A theory of action is a model that explains how specific actions or strategies will lead to desired outcomes. It outlines the causal relationships between what is done (inputs or interventions) and the expected results (outcomes or impacts). In essence, it provides a roadmap for achieving goals by identifying the steps and mechanisms that are thought to drive success.

A Theory of Action for our example Instructional Vision might be:

> If members of the Instructional Leadership Team (ILT) strengthen their capacity to improve teaching and learning by enhancing their own pedagogical knowledge and skills, then they will be able to provide more effective, standards-aligned, and intentional instruction across the school.

> If ILT members focus on the development of durable skills across all grade levels and abandon misaligned technology and practices, then they will foster a healthier learning environment that better supports student growth and engagement.

If the ILT implements a continuous cycle of professional development, reflective practice, and collaboration, then they will empower teachers to refine their instructional strategies, leading to higher-quality teaching and improved student outcomes.

Ultimately, the combination of improved leadership capacity, targeted skill development, and a focus on sustainable instructional practices will contribute to a more effective learning environment where students are better prepared for long-term academic success.

Responsibilities and Actions by Role

Once goals are formalized, each member of the educational team has responsibilities and actions aligned with the annual goals:

- » What does the District Team do?
- » What do the Principals and Assistant Principals do?
- » What do the Site Leadership Teams do?
- » What do the Teachers do?
- » What do the Students do?
- » What do the Parents do?

Attaching each team member's responsibility to the goal provides clarity and purpose. This is distributed leadership in action. Each member helped to develop the goal and can clearly see their role in supporting its attainment.

The chart on the following page provides an example of how a district planning team might communicate the roles and responsibilities for an Annual Goal.

Annual Goal	Instructional Leadership Team (ILT) members will strengthen their capacity to improve teaching and learning. They will accomplish this by improving their pedagogical knowledge and skills and focusing on standards-aligned intentional instruction. They will foster a healthy environment through the strategic abandonment of misaligned technology and practices, and will focus on the development of durable skills at all grade levels.
Role	**Responsibilities and Actions**
District Team	» Provide opportunities for principals and ILT members to unpack, understand, and use content standards. » Ensure that an ongoing Professional Development Plan is implemented on Intentional Teaching and Durable Skill development for all teachers. » Conduct a district-wide audit of technology using the Technology Filter Tool. » Develop/provide Parent Education programs on Intentional Teaching and Durable Skills.
Principal and Assistant Principal	» Provide opportunities for ILT members to lead all teachers through the process of unpacking, understanding, and using content standards. » Ensure that all teachers attend Professional Development on Intentional Teaching and Durable Skills development. » Ensure that ILT members participate in a district-wide audit of technology using the Technology Filter Tool. » Develop/provide Parent Education programs on Intentional Teaching and Durable Skills.
Instructional Leadership Team	» Lead grade-level or content-level teachers through the process of unpacking, understanding, and using content standards. » Attend Professional Development on Intentional Teaching and Durable Skills development. » Participate in a district-wide audit of technology using the Technology Filter Tool.
Teacher Teams	» Participate in the process of unpacking, understanding, and using content standards. » Attend Professional Development on Intentional Teaching and Durable Skills development. » Provide input during the district-wide audit of technology using the Technology Filter Tool.
Teachers	» Use your knowledge of content standards, Intentional Teaching, and Durable Skills to develop robust lessons and activities for students. » Attend Professional Development on Intentional Teaching and Durable Skills development. » Provide input during the district-wide audit of technology using the Technology Filter Tool.
Students	» Work to master Content Standards and Durable Skills because of rigorous Intentional Instruction.
Parents	» Ensure children attend school every day. » Limit screen time during out-of-school hours. » Attend Parent Education programs offered by the district and schools.

The roles provided in the table are examples. Districts must address the roles that are appropriate for their organization.

Roles that may be included are:

» Academic coaches
» Intervention teachers
» Counselors
» Classified staff
» After-school staff
» PTA, Booster Clubs, or other parent support groups

The key to this part of the Instructional Vision is to ensure that the people who are responsible for achieving the goal understand their assigned tasks. In this way, the entire organization is working in tandem toward the intended outcomes.

Here we need to revisit the fact that Distributed Leadership does not abolish a district or site administrator of their responsibility to ensure all members of the organization are completing their required responsibilities. District and site leaders should be aware of the expectations of each member of their team and establish a system for check-ins to keep everyone moving forward.

Check-ins can be as simple as a brief discussion at regularly scheduled meetings (e.g., staff meetings) addressing progress toward the goal, using the roles and responsibility chart as an anchoring tool. Check-ins can be more structured, such as bi-monthly meetings with individuals. The system that a leader puts in place should be realistic based on the available time and the needs of their team. Teams requiring more support should have more frequent check-ins.

> Check-ins can be as simple as a brief discussion at regularly scheduled meetings or be more structured, such as bi-monthly meetings with individuals.

Metrics for Success and Ongoing Evaluation of Goals

During the development of the Instructional Vision, districts need to consider what conditions are needed for the Instructional Vision to be successful. Has the vision document clearly articulated the who, what, when, and how components of the Instructional Vision? Does the plan provide clear guidance on what would constitute a successful implementation?

To monitor the effectiveness of our actions, metrics must be developed. Metrics for Success are driven by the intended goals, district structures, and outcomes. The key to this process is to clearly define what needs to be measured and to define the indicators of success.

There are many ways for an organization to develop this section of its Instructional Vision.

Meeting the district where it currently operates and building from there is a solid way to begin this process. Metrics for Success can be simple or more complex depending on the needs of the district; however, they must include short-term metrics, long-term outcomes, and ongoing evaluation tools.

Short-term metrics might include using formative assessments and walk-through data each quarter. Long-term outcomes would be assessed with summative measures, such as graduation rates, state testing data, and district benchmarks.

Ongoing evaluation tools should include a detailed progress monitoring schedule and data review cycles.

Supporting Information

The final component of the Instructional Vision is the inclusion of supporting documents. The documents selected for this section of the Instructional Vision should be chosen for their ability to provide further clarification on expectations.

Documents that are recommended for inclusion are:

» Model School Day samples
» Annual Professional Learning Plan
» Technology Filter

Model School Day

Model School Day samples provide school principals and classroom teachers with clarity for the use of instructional time. In an elementary school program, the documents provide the expected number of instructional minutes by content area. The Model School Day provides specificity for grade levels, with guidance about the number of minutes and how to structure specific content areas for time spent on the various components within that content.

For example, within Language Arts, the Model Day might delineate the amount of time for Foundational Skills, Comprehension, and Writing, etc. A Model School Day for a Middle or High School outlines the expectations for the Master Schedule (traditional, block, etc.) and might also include specificity for content areas, as well. Model School Day documents must include the amount of time that students should be engaging in screen time, specific to each grade level.

It is important to note that the Model School Day documents are provided as guidelines and are not lock-step directives that must be adhered to in a manner that would hinder teachers from making sound instructional decisions. They provide an exemplar for what a school day should look like in a perfect world.

Annual Professional Learning Plan

The inclusion of the Annual Professional Learning Plan demonstrates the cohesiveness of the work.

It lays out the dates, times, audience, and purpose of the intended professional learning events.

Anyone reading the Instructional Vision should see a clear link between the Annual Goals and the Professional Learning activities included in the plan. For each area of the Annual Goal, a comprehensive professional learning plan should be developed. A sample of what should be included for each area of professional learning is provided below.

Intentional Teaching Professional Development Plan	
Dates	August 12; October 21; February 24
Time	8:00am — 3:00pm
Audience	High School Math and Science Teachers
Location	Multi-Purpose Room at High School
Purpose	Introduction to and ongoing support for Intentional Teaching. Participants will develop a common language and plan lessons using the Intentional Teaching Framework
Intended Outcomes	Participants learn the why, when, and how to plan and deliver Intentional Teaching lessons
Professional Learning Lead	Consultant
Funding Source	Title 1
Total Cost	$45,000 which includes substitute teacher costs

Technology Filter

Including the Technology Filter in the Instructional Vision is crucial to the alignment of instructional minutes for technology use as outlined in the Model School Day documents. Principals and teachers will use the Technology Filter to make informed decisions about the use of technology in each classroom. The development of the Technology Filter is discussed in detail in Chapter 4.

Instructional Leadership Team Model

Developing the Instructional Leadership Team model takes a commitment to teamwork, and while the initial work to get the system functioning can seem daunting, it is important to focus on the result. A team that wishes to embark on this journey should focus on getting the process started, not on perfection, because built into this model is a constant cycle of analysis and refinement.

Once the system is established, the work of the ILT becomes increasingly focused on teaching and learning.

On the following page is a sample timeline for the Instructional Leadership model.

Instructional Leadership Team - Sample timeline

Planning Team	District ILT Meetings	Site ILT
Summer	**Early Fall, Winter, Spring**	**Fall, Winter, Spring** (2-3 meetings each season following the District ILT Meetings)
Led by: Superintendent and/or Assistant Superintendent of Educational Services, with the support of an Educational Consultant.	**Led by:** Superintendent and/or Assistant Superintendent of Educational Services, with the support of an Educational Consultant.	**Led by:** Principal and Site ILT
District Leadership assembles a Planning Team by selecting key representatives from the following groups: • District Administrators • Principals and Assistant Principals • Association/Union Leadership • Teachers • Parent Association Leadership • Student Leaders (usually Middle or High School) Planning Team meets 1-3 times to: • Analyze relevant data • Write the Instructional Vision Statement • Determine the Instructional Framework • Develop the Annual Goals (Years 1-5) • Develop the criteria for success (metrics)	District Leadership sets the schedule for these meetings prior to the school year beginning and communicates these dates with all district and site leadership. District Leadership plans for the meeting (develops agenda and prepares all materials). District Leadership handles logistics per district protocol (e.g. confirming room, securing substitutes, planning for refreshments, etc.). Principals ensure that all Site ILT members are prepared to attend the meeting.	Principal schedules Site ILT meetings to follow each District ILT and communicates these dates to all Site ILT members. During Site ILT meetings, the Principal and Site ILT plan for school site meetings (staff meetings, collaboration, etc.) to cover key information regarding the Instructional Vision and steps to take toward the annual goals.

Annual Summer Retreats

Planning Team meets 1-3 times to: • Analyze relevant data in relationship to the criteria for success (metrics) • Review the Instructional Vision Statement • Review Instructional Framework • Update the Annual Goals (Years 2-5)	Site ILT meets 1-2 times to: • Analyze site data • Review progress toward annual goals • Plan Site ILT meetings for upcoming school year

When thinking about the compounding challenges schools face, including declining job satisfaction, the decoupling of education from physical spaces, the reduction of social interaction, and a myopic overuse of technology, focusing our leadership on a clearly articulated plan is a crucial step toward schools redefining what a quality public education can offer.

The Instructional Vision document outlines a comprehensive approach to ensuring student success through a well-defined plan of action. At its core, the Instructional Vision prioritizes student-centered learning aligned with clear, pedagogical, research-based practices. Through collaboration and teamwork, and the identified core values, this process provides the blueprint for all decision-making and actions within the educational community. Using the Instructional Vision document as a living roadmap is the key to success. The development of this plan is not an act of compliance that is completed and then left on the shelf. The power of the plan is that it is widely distributed both in print and online and referenced daily. Every meeting, discussion, or professional learning event should start with a reference to the plan. This ensures everyone is clear on where the team is and knows their role in the work.

Chapter 3
Developing a Common Language
of
Intentional Instruction

The hardest assumption to challenge is the one you don't even know you are making.[1]

-Douglas Adams

 Author of The Hitchhiker's Guide to the Galaxy

High-performing schools and districts have a common, coherent, calibrated language of standards-based instruction.

That is not a controversial statement. Whether the research that supports this statement is Robert Marzano's work,[2] or the extensive research around 90-90-90 schools dating back almost thirty years,[3] or more recent work, such as that by The New Teacher Project,[4] there is no substantial body of research claiming the opposite. There is broad agreement that highly effective schools—regardless of socio-economic status, levels of multilingualism, or other variables not controlled by the school systems—have welcoming and safe environments, a common language of instruction, grade level standards-based expectations, and professionals actively collaborating on curriculum, data, and the actual practice of teaching.

If the formula is broadly known, why is it not broadly implemented? The answer lies in the Adams quote above. The hardest assumptions to overcome are the ones that we don't even know we are making. An enduring truth in our work with schools is that the part of a school's instructional program that most often gets assumed is that everyone agrees on what instruction looks like. And even more so that there is agreement on what quality, standards-based instruction looks like. In a book about the dangers of screen-based instruction and the isolated learning that it promotes, this chapter is

necessary because a core tenet to operationalize an instructional vision—the work of Chapter Two—is developing a coherent instructional program that supports that vision. That is impossible when everyone—teacher, principal, superintendent— is using the same terminology with different meanings.
In working with hundreds of schools for more than three decades, four core reasons repeatedly surface that shed light on why the language of instruction is so disjointed:

1. There is no agreed-upon body of work upon which instructional practices rest or can be traced back to. This is not because there hasn't been rigorous work on the science of learning or instructional practices that most effectively align with how the brain learns, but because fads, silver bullets, and strong opinions are frequently given the same currency as research-based methodologies.
2. There is little consistency in the content or quality of teacher preparation programs, within and across states.
3. The implementation of professional development tends to be scattered, optional, and not followed up with a systematic rollout and feedback loops.
4. The classroom doors are rarely breached. Once a teacher is given their own classroom, they can go entire careers without observing other teachers. The ability to learn from each other is reduced to conversations at best in professional learning community settings (PLCs), and more often in teachers' lounges. These conversations are told from a single perspective on what is happening in the teacher's own specific classroom.

This chapter is not about instruction per se. Rather, it is about how imperative it is to develop a common language that will serve as a prism or a filter for what makes its way into the classroom.

Saying that education does not have a common language is not the same thing as saying there isn't a common vernacular. A common vernacular does exist. Most educators would agree on the need to use "best practices," for example. What those practices look like when operationalized is where the inconsistency comes in. Examples abound about different interpretations of the same concept, even though every individual element of instruction that is mentioned in this chapter- whether "Learning Objective" or "Modeling" or "Concept Development"—has had whole books devoted to it, or substantial chapters in broader books about instructional frameworks, such Madeline Hunter's *Mastery Teaching* or Gene Tavernetti's *Teach Fast.*[56]

For illustrative purposes, consider the term "checking for understanding," which Douglas Fisher and Nancy Frey wrote about back in 2007.[7] Everyone in a department meeting, grade level meeting, or PLC would nod and agree that checking for understanding is important. As Fisher and Frey take great pains to point out, though, many of the standard practices that get lumped under "checking for understanding" are checking for participation, engagement, affirmation, or the student's opinion on whether she understands. Asking "Does anyone have any questions?" or "Is everyone with me?" might invite a brave few souls to pose a relevant question, but it doesn't provide actionable, formative data that a teacher can use in the moment to make instructional decisions. And that is, at its core, what checking for understanding is: the systematic gathering of actionable data with which a teacher can make informed decisions to go forward, or pivot as needed.

That definition seems straightforward enough, but ask a group of administrators or teachers to share what checking for understanding is, and the answers in the same school will vary widely. Some sample responses:

» "My students use individual whiteboards to show their responses so I can gather whole class data immediately."
» "Show me Fist to Five. Fist, if you don't understand at all, and five if you've got this."
» "I ask a question, pause to let students process and know that they are accountable, then select non-volunteers to give me authentic data."
» "Show me a thumbs up if you understand."
» "I check for understanding on Thursdays, after I've taught for a couple of days."

Those statements are not all equally valid. Some statements are authentically gauging where students are, while others are gauging where students feel they are. It is as if we are using the same words, but in different dialects. The same variance extends to other lesson elements such as "activating prior knowledge," "guided practice," and "closure." And these examples are from direct instruction methodology, with its deep and lengthy research base. The variance when discussing indirect instruction methods such as inquiry or discovery-based models is even greater, as those methods tend to get less attention in teacher preparation programs.

> Schools must take careful steps to develop a shared language of instruction that includes more than listing terms or definitions.

To combat these misunderstandings, schools must take careful steps to develop a shared language of instruction that includes more than listing terms or definitions. The work involves providing examples, non-examples, and models. Moreover, schools must develop a shared understanding of what that language looks like when operationalized during effective instruction by providing opportunities to observe and discuss teaching and learning, a critical step in the calibration process.[8]

Education is one of the few professions that does not have a canonical body of work to refer to for common guidance. In the study of medicine, law, architecture, accounting, real estate, and the like, there are commonly accepted beliefs and principles that drive the practice. As these beliefs and principles evolve, continuing education and certification ensure that practitioners evolve along with them.

The same cannot be said for education. What "teaching" and "teacher preparation" mean, state to state, university to university, program to program, is a patchwork quilt, as demonstrated by recent research by WestEd.[9] There are several states that require a fifth year of undergraduate education to obtain a teaching credential, after completion of a bachelor's degree. Meanwhile, several states do not require a bachelor's degree and certify teachers with just sixty credits of undergraduate education. While states and districts with teacher shortages cannot be faulted for trying to find alternative pathways to staff schools, it does raise the important question of how differences in understanding are bridged once the teachers are hired and placed in a classroom.

Within the actual program of study, the requirements for clinical experience and course requirements also varied widely by state, and the expectations within states are not substantially more consistent. In California, for example, there are more than two hundred institutions and pathways for an individual to receive a teaching credential. There is little congruence on the quality of the pathway or program, although the credential that is conveyed is the same, and with it, the assumption that what it means to teach is commonly understood. And then in August or September, or mid-year, those new teachers are placed in classrooms side by side after a few days of induction or new teacher training, possibly with opposing notions of core instructional elements. Whereas one new teacher had student teaching experience and a master teacher who provided formative feedback on direct instruction methodology, the second only took eight-week online courses with no practicum, and the third had a master teacher who dabbled in the "flipped classroom" and other inquiry-based methods. How will those new teachers calibrate?

Unless a school district, a building principal, or an Instructional Leadership Team makes the overt, concerted effort to arrive at some common understanding, what often results is a hodgepodge of instructional practices that bear little resemblance to each other.

Common terms are assumed to mean the same thing when the only thing they have in common from classroom to classroom is that the terms are used loosely, and everyone nods in agreement.

A clear Instructional Vision begins with a shared understanding of what high-quality teaching looks like—defining the instructional model and establishing the verbiage that everyone will use. To shape this vision meaningfully, teams must dig into thoughtful conversations about the pedagogical approaches they value, the evolving role of technology, and, importantly, what is known about how the brain learns. These insights don't just refine the instructional model; they help design learning experiences that are structured, intentional, and aligned with how students process, retain, and apply information.

The Science of Learning

In Chapter 1 we discussed the impact that screen time outside of school is having on children and the way in which excessive classroom-based screen time is impacting key learning skills. A logical place then for a school district to begin its work in developing a common language of instruction is around how the brain processes information, and how these processes can either be enhanced or disrupted, whether by humans or technology.

Teacher preparation programs generally spend very little time on cognitive science. This is unfortunate because education is likely the only profession that tries to impact a specific human organ without substantially knowing how that organ works. Compare that to an ophthalmologist who doesn't spend years learning the structure and processes of the eye, or a cardiologist who doesn't spend years learning the structure and processes of the heart.

Fortunately for educators, there is much new research being done in the field of the science of learning, and also, fortunately for educators, they don't need to know everything about the brain in order to develop lessons that are "brain-compatible." In the early part of this century, we developed an instructional framework called the FAST (Focused, Adaptable, Structured Teaching) Framework, built largely on a direct instruction base and three texts: *Teaching With the Brain in Mind* by Eric Jensen, *How the Brain Learns* by David Sousa, and *Brain Rules* by John Medina."[10][11][12] The FAST Framework has been used for two decades by hundreds of schools and thousands of teachers as a simple yet comprehensive way of structuring lessons.

The FAST Framework, or any framework eventually adopted by a school or district in its process of developing a common language of instruction, benefits from the use of a few key concepts from the science of learning:

» Attention Span Limits
» Primacy Recency
» Cognitive Load
» Retrieval Practice through Repetitions

These concepts help to guide the lesson structure in a way that makes sense for students and doesn't overwhelm student brains.

In 1999, before the explosion of social media, before the ubiquity of the internet, Jean Healy, in her important book, *Endangered Minds: Why Our Children Don't Think,*[13] reported on how children's brains were being rewired as a response to changing media. At the time, the main culprits were video games, music videos, and other media that children consumed. Healy described the quick-moving action in video games that children responded to and the way music videos were edited. Newer music videos, for example, looked very different from earlier generations of music videos. The original videos were two to four-minute "stories" that followed the lyrics of the songs. The next generation of videos was a completely new genre. Each scene seemed random, and the edits were very quick, many times with multiple cuts and different scenes appearing within a matter of seconds. This reflected a broader trend across entertainment and gaming, with rapidly intensifying inputs.

The physiology of individual brains changed to accommodate the changing, fast-paced environment. New neural pathways were created in order to adapt. And as a result of their rewired brain, students' attention spans decreased. The ability to think deeply about any topic was impaired as students' ability to attend to any task for long periods of time was diminished.

Since Healy's work, what has been done to mitigate this rewiring?

Nothing.

It has been exacerbated. Videos, posts, and reels promote quick scrolling and clicking. Many teachers have surrendered to these changes and turned to instruction by screens as well, under the belief that using a medium that is used outside of school for entertainment will help students thrive in school as well, perhaps forgetting Marshall McLuhan's warning that the medium is the message.[14] Students who are used to turning to screens for entertainment will only turn to that medium for learning if some of the same attributes that made it entertaining are present, including gamification, instant gratification, and intense, quick action. In the absence of those attributes, students are more likely to *disengage* when the medium of instruction is a screen, as borne out by more than 500 classroom observations in grades kinder through 12 during the writing of this book. In fact, the mere act of having an open screen during instruction led to lower levels of engagement, even when the teacher was the one providing the instruction, an observation borne out by research cited in Chapter 1 that the mere presence of a screen tended to result in lower student retention.

There is a bolder way to face the current reality of children and the changes that are occurring in their brains. That is by using the available evidence to provide instruction that provides the best opportunities for all students to succeed. In developing a common language of instruction, educators must understand the challenges described above and incorporate known insights into how students learn, gleaned from research in cognitive science, cognitive psychology, and other areas pertinent to teaching and learning.

Limited Attention Spans

Students' ability to attend to schoolwork has diminished in recent years. Whether that is by choice or because of physiological rewiring, the reality that human beings, and children in particular, have limited attention spans is nothing new. The statement, "human beings have limited attention spans," will evoke yawns and "you don't say" reactions from classroom teachers.

While research on students' attention spans has yet to provide definitive, exact time limits that students can attend to schoolwork, observations of students will quickly tell us that the time is finite.[15] Generally, the younger the child, the shorter the time they can attend. Some authors suggest teachers use a ten-minute rule for students of all ages. Others suggest teachers use one minute per year of age as a guideline. For example, if a student is seven years old, the average length of time a student may attend is seven minutes.

Teachers know they do not need peer-reviewed research to tell them their students have a limited attention span. Teachers can see it in their students' eyes. They can see it in student fidgeting. They can see it, feel it, when the limits to the students' attention have been reached. Students' ability to pay attention comes from how their bodies and minds interact with what's happening around them — which is why lessons need to be well-structured and designed in ways that keep students actively responsible for their learning.

While planning and delivering instruction, a good rule of thumb regarding students' attention spans is that it is better to assume a shorter span of time than a longer one. A bigger, more applicable rule of thumb that applies to all areas of life is, "When someone is done listening, be done talking."

Cognitive Load Theory

Teachers might question how to use information on limited attention spans in lesson planning: "How in the world can I teach a lesson in ten or fifteen minutes?" It is important in the conversations around instruction to note that attention spans are not the only variable impacting students' ability to process information. Another variable with a robust research base to consider in designing and delivering lessons is cognitive load. Cognitive load theory refers to the amount of new information, or "chunks" of information, that can be processed in working memory at one time. When new content is introduced in a lesson, it adds to the cognitive load, which can either support or overwhelm students' ability to absorb and retain the material.

How much new information can be stored in working memory depends on several factors.

In cognitive load theory, there are three types of cognitive load: intrinsic, germane, and extraneous loads. Intrinsic load is determined by the complexity of the content and the learner's experience as it relates to new information. Germane load is the necessary load that must be shouldered by working memory to construct schemas and transfer information into long-term memory. Extraneous load is unnecessary load that does not lead to the retention of information. Instructional practices, classroom environment, and materials either minimize or maximize cognitive load.[16]

The teacher must take control and own all three types of cognitive load during a lesson. For example, when determining the learning objective for any lesson, teachers must consider the amount of new content to be presented—intrinsic load. Teachers must also consider the amount of background knowledge and necessary prior skills to teach the new content— germane load. And finally, the teacher must protect the student from unnecessary distractions—extraneous load—that could contribute to increased cognitive load.

Mitigating the first two loads described above seems obvious. Intrinsic load is managed by the teacher performing a task analysis on the new content: What do I want the students to know or do? What do they know now? Is the objective too much? Should I teach a smaller chunk of content? How will I break down the content to make it accessible?

Germane load is similarly tackled through a task analysis for specific points in a lesson: How can students' prior knowledge be accessed in a way that will help this new content make sense? What vocabulary, graphic organizer, or subskill that students already know do I need to help them retrieve to reduce the intrinsic load? What real-life application or example can be shared to help provide a mental schema?

The third load—extraneous cognitive load—is sneakier. Medina's *Brain Rules* captures the difficulty of combating extraneous cognitive load: "The expert forgets what it's like to be a novice."[17] In teaching content about which the teacher is passionate, it can be very easy to load a lesson with extraneous details, which can crowd out the main point for the novice. Medina urges big idea first, details later, and to make sure that the details don't overwhelm the big idea.

One of us witnessed a wonderful example of this during a visit to a Revolutionary War era cemetery on Boston's Freedom Trail. A teacher standing next to Paul Revere's grave was explaining to 5th-grade students on a field trip about his famous ride to warn the Minutemen about the British attack. She spoke excitedly about the window in the old North Church, the lanterns that would be deployed there, the saying "one if by sea, two if by land," and the route that the riders were to take. Then a student raised her hand to interrupt and asked, "But, who won the war?"

The expert forgets what it's like to be a novice.

Extraneous load also occurs outside of the lesson itself. Extraneous cognitive load results from environmental overload, such as lawn mowing, announcements on the intercom precisely at the wrong times, and a noisy classroom next door. These external sources of extraneous cognitive load, along with some that teachers might bring themselves, such as a messy classroom, overdone decorations, and whiteboards crowded with announcements, all contribute to student distraction.

Primacy-Recency

A core concept that should also be considered in developing a common language of instruction is how time is used within a learning episode. This has its roots in the primacy-recency, or serial position effect, first coined by Hermann Ebbinghaus in the 19th century. This effect, the result of over thirty years of Ebbinghaus meticulously recording his own memory and memory lapses, has since been supported by hundreds of follow-up studies and shows that students generally learn best what is taught first in a learning episode and second best what is taught last in a learning episode.[18]

The most effective time to teach the important new content so that students encode the content into working memory is the beginning of the learning episode, primacy. An effective time for retrieval and consolidation of the new content is at the end of the lesson, recency.

There are many implications of Primacy-Recency to be considered: When is homework corrected? When are activities scheduled within a learning block of time? When are announcements made over the intercom system? There are also lesson-specific implications about how to activate prior knowledge, why it is so important to model cleanly before students are asked to perform a task, and how to close a lesson to increase retention.

Considering Primacy-Recency, Cognitive Load Theory, and Attention Span Limits Together

The implications for lesson design and instruction are clear: the most important content in the lesson should be presented at the beginning of the lesson and retrieved or reviewed at the end of the lesson. Coupling this concept with the limits on attention span and cognitive load limits, one can start to see the outline of what an Instructional Leadership Team might arrive at as its common lesson framework:

The first seven to fifteen minutes of a learning episode are spent on the most important new learning, with the major concept to be attained receiving the bulk of the attention. The new learning has an appropriate intrinsic cognitive load that the learner can make sense of. This learning happens with the support of germane cognitive load, which helps the learner retrieve prior learning and create some schema for the new learning to "hang" on. During this time, the extraneous cognitive load, like collecting homework and making announcements, is severely limited or eliminated.

The final ten to twelve minutes of a learning episode are spent on a second major concept or on consolidating the information from the first fifteen minutes. In the FAST lesson framework, the "recency" part of the learning episode is spent on the end of guided practice and a beefy closure, in which students explain what they learned, the importance of the concept or skill, and how to complete the task, if applicable.

In between the primacy and recency peaks, what Sousa called the "downtime," students spend time rehearsing the new content, whether the content be solving math problems or identifying symbolism in poetry passages, or fleshing out the details of a big idea presented during the first fifteen minutes, such as how carbon cycles through Earth's spheres. [19]

Retrieval and Repetitions

A final Science of Learning concept to be considered, also initially the courtesy of Ebbinghaus, is the need for carefully constructed and timed retrieval of new learning. Learning, especially classroom learning, does not happen and "stick" after one iteration. Rather, the new learning needs to be consciously retrieved several times for it to migrate from working memory, where it first resides, into long-term memory. The number of times that a specific piece of learning needs to be rehearsed to be moved into long-term memory will vary based on complexity and its intrinsic cognitive load, but Marzano's research showed that a new skill or concept practiced between 18 and 24 times could fairly reliably be retrieved by most learners.[20]

A key to the repetitions is that they must be spaced out, with increasingly longer intervals between repetitions, the further the learner gets from the original learning. An important consideration when deciding how students will practice content is whether the practice is naive or deliberate. Anders Ericsson makes clear that not all practice is created equal. [21] He establishes an important distinction between what he calls naive practice and deliberate practice. Naive practice might be thought of as engagement with content. Think of a child who loves to play soccer and is on the pitch multiple hours every day playing with his friends. The child may generally improve, but the improvement will be much slower than if she had practiced with a coach. The child could play day after day and never learn to dribble better because she is dribbling well enough to have fun, or might only dribble with the preferred foot, rather than both feet. On the other hand, if she had been practicing with a coach, the coach would have provided opportunities to practice specifically and deliberately, with feedback using drills that focused on the specific parts of dribbling in which the girl needed to practice. Students are no different from most adults; they want to practice those things in which they are already proficient and leave improvement in other skills for another day.

Similarly, the spaced, or distributed, practice must be specific and deliberate. Although some content within a school year, particularly in math instruction, builds on past learning, often the subsequent practice that is built into future learning objectives is not sufficiently deliberate to help the move into long-term memory. Specific, deliberate retrieval of the content to be ingrained is necessary. In other content areas, especially those that jump from topic to topic over the course of the year, such as history or biology, the incidental mention of a piece of past learning in the context of new learning is also not deliberate enough to "count" towards the necessary number of repetitions.

We worked with a high school principal years ago whose teachers were balking at the notion of implementing the distributed practice of past learning into their daily plans. He asked, "So what exactly needs to be put into this distributed practice rotation?" Our response: "Just whatever you want them to remember."

One last note on repetitions and practice. Marzano's research on practice also showed that the great bulk of learning new content comes from the first six to eight repetitions.[22] As a district, an ILT, or a school team works on its common language of instruction, an important conversation to have is how much work is assigned and when. In an environment where student attention span and task persistence are growing concerns, does it make sense to assign more than six to eight repetitions of independent practice or homework if the first six or eight are where the bulk of learning happens? Better to let students focus on six or eight problems or passages and have a better chance of practicing correctly.

The Limits Guide the Structure: Developing a Common Language of Instruction

Earlier, we described an environment in which educators are rightly concerned about students' shortened attention spans, fragmentation of focus, lack of task persistence, and disengagement. All of those have gotten worse since you started to read this book, and certainly in the time it has taken us to write it. The persistent and pernicious use of individualized screens in the last decade has had negative impacts on many elements of memory and focus that are readily apparent in classroom-based learning. Human limits should drive what teaching and learning should look like, but that has always been the case. Human brains did not evolve to listen to hour-long lectures or to adapt to a constant stream of tidbits of information. Those limits should guide the structure of what instruction looks like, and a district or ILT should make the limits from the last few pages a central consideration as it begins to wrestle with these questions:

» What does an effective lesson look like?
» If it isn't a lesson, what do we call it?
» Is a "three-day lesson" acceptable? (The science of learning would say no: break it up into three one-day lessons.)
» How much practice should be assigned, and when should it happen?
» Does the use of individualized screens, especially during primacy-recency, augment the learning or replace the human instruction?
» When is content purposefully revisited to provide additional, necessary repetitions?

These conversations—grounded in what we know about how the brain learns best—are at the heart of developing a common language of instruction. There is no way that the three teachers discussed earlier from three different teacher preparation programs can have the same responses without a concerted effort to develop a common understanding.

Evidence-Based, Evergreen Practices

As mentioned earlier, there is no comprehensive canon of work that all new teachers are introduced to before starting service. Fortunately for educators, much is known about how to operationalize the science of how the brain learns into lesson design.

In 2012, educational psychologist Barak Rosenshine published research on effective instruction, now known as Rosenshine's Principles.[23] He developed the principles based on evidence in cognitive science, classroom observations, and other empirical studies.

These ten principles addressed three areas important to teaching and learning:

» How people learn and acquire new information.
» How master teachers implement classroom strategies.
» How teachers can support students while learning complex information.

The strength and validity of the principles come from classroom observations of teachers and students. As the principles are listed and explained, they seem so self-evident that educators will find them evergreen and non-controversial.

Rosenshine's Ten Principles of Effective Instruction:

1. Begin each lesson with a short review of prior learning.
2. Present new material in small steps followed by practice.
3. Ask questions and check for students' responses.
4. Provide models and examples.
5. Guided student practice activities.
6. Monitor student comprehension.
7. Aim for a high success rate.
8. Scaffold difficult tasks.
9. Require and monitor independent practice.
10. Engage students in weekly and monthly reviews.

Rosenshine's ten principles provide a blueprint for the design of effective teaching and learning. Educators will notice how Rosenshine's ten principles closely align with elements of other teacher-directed lesson designs. There is strong overlap with the work cited earlier by Marzano, Hunter, and the FAST Framework, pre-dating Rosenshine's work, as well as the science of learning of Sousa, Medina, Jensen, and others.

In each body of work, successful instruction can be broken down into three or four major "chunks", whether those chunks be labeled "I do, We do, You do" or "Review Material, Question, Sequence Concepts and Model, Stages of Practice" or some other variation. [24]

Comparison of Rosenshine's Principles
With Direct Instruction Lesson Elements

Rosenshine	Lesson Elements
Begin each lesson with a short review of prior learning	Activate prior knowledge
Present new material in small chunks and practice	Concept Development
Ask questions and ask for students' responses	Continuous Check for Understanding
Provide models and examples.	Modeling
Guided student practice activities	Guided practice
Monitor student comprehension	Throughout the lesson
Aim for student success	Criteria for success during each element of the lesson determines the next step
Scaffold a difficult task	Step-by-step model and Guided Practice
Require and monitor independent practice	Independent Practice
Engage students in weekly and monthly reviews	Outside of the lesson, if not critical for the new lesson

A copy of our FAST Framework, along with sample lessons, can be found in the book's online notes section: schoolsnext.

org/digital-captives-notes. The framework captures each of the elements listed above, but schools do not have to implement our specific instructional framework to experience the positive impacts of Rosenshine's Ten Principles. Other frameworks do similar work. What a school or district cannot do is "pick and choose." The ultimate goal should be to establish all necessary effective practices as part of a cohesive instructional program aligned with the school or district's agreed-upon vision.

And to do this, schools or districts need to be much more selective about what professional development is brought into the building: if it doesn't align with the instructional vision, resources—both financial and more importantly, teachers' time—will not be allocated to it. Too often, professional development is a series of "one-and-done" workshops, where teachers are told to pick a strategy or two they want to implement with little follow-up support or coaching. This is in direct opposition to the notion of developing a common language of instruction.

Consider Rosenshine's Principles. Picture that one teacher attended the workshop and decided to try "Aim for student success" and "Monitor student comprehension," but didn't change their instruction in a meaningful way. Their colleague in the classroom next door chose to focus on "Provide models and examples" and "Guided student practice activities," which did impact the actual delivery of instruction. When asked by their principal what they thought of the workshop a month later, they might have widely diverging opinions of how useful the professional development offering was. One teacher might report that students made noticeable improvements with clear models and guided practice, while the other might note that students showed no progress, despite her efforts to achieve student success. And as often happens, Rosenshine's work might then be relegated to the dustbin of "well, use it if it works for you," with one teacher possibly continuing the practice while the other abandons it.

Schools need to consider professional development in total when deciding where to spend their teachers' time. From our experience, teachers have a right to be cynical about not enough forethought being given to their training. School leaders frequently chase the latest book they read or conference they attended, without sufficient planning and thought given to the actual incremental implementation. Implementing pieces might help in a piecemeal fashion, but developing a comprehensive, cohesive instructional program through professional development requires tying in what and how teachers are trained to the instructional vision. To achieve this, a school district must incorporate the principles in its overarching goals and indicate the incremental steps to improving teaching and learning across each year of the plan.

The Difficult Work of Developing a Common Language of Instruction

Schools and districts, especially in this post-COVID-19, post-screen time explosion, are in vastly different places. While some who did substantial work around developing a common language of instruction are doing well, many have turned instruction over to screens. In the absence of fundamental agreements around what constitutes instruction, many have fallen prey to using online programs and platforms that were designed as supplements as their core instruction.

Because there are different starting points, the listed set of steps below is not numbered, but each step is critical and needs to be completed in an order that makes sense to move towards a common language.

- » Develop an instructional leadership team (ILT) composed of a representative sample of stakeholders who will be impacted by the ILT's policy decisions
- » Build consensus through research on at least three key areas:
  - » Overuse of technology and its impacts
  - » The science of learning
  - » Effective lesson design
- » Reach consensus on five to seven core instructional principles based on research, not opinions

» Adopt a comprehensive framework of instruction that captures the core principles, with written definitions, examples, and non-examples, and the justification for each
» Align professional development for each necessary staff group (administrators, teachers, coaches, and new teachers)
» Develop a list of actionable steps with a timetable
» Learn to say no
» Cull away distractions that steal teachers' and students' time
» Develop markers of success
» Gradually introduce or reintroduce agreed-upon individual strategies into the now-established framework

The process involves several phases focused on key ideas around best practices in instruction and the science of learning, and guides teams in creating a common and shared instructional language centered on research-based tenets. The process will encourage participants to engage with research, reflect on key questions, and build consensus on what effective instruction looks like in their school district.

Whether the leader of the process is an ILT, a principal, or a superintendent, it is critical to discuss the essential research-based components of effective instruction with stakeholder groups. This common understanding of the "why" is essential to reaching a consensus on a common language of instruction that aligns with the Instructional Vision developed in Chapter 2. The development of a common language ensures that there are agreed-upon ideas across the district on effective teaching practices, essential skills, and how students learn best. This language will also guide the school or district in developing aligned professional development.

Learn to Say No

A subset of the process of developing a common instructional language in a school or district is occasionally saying no, at times even to productive practices. The key, stressed in Marzano's work, is the emphasis on adopting a framework for instruction first.[25] Many individual strategies produce benefits, but the first precondition for having a calibrated, coherent language of instruction is having somewhere to nest the strategies, rather than implementing individual strategies in the absence of a coordinating framework.

A good example of this is engaging students in structured student talk. Engaging students in academic discourse is important. Students will not use the language of the content they are learning outside of the classroom, and so it is a practice that should be encouraged and practiced in class. That said, we have seen schools and districts make "academic discourse" their overriding goal for a school year, in the absence of a coherent instructional framework. This results in a disjointed implementation of student talk that is eventually abandoned. Inconsistent answers to questions like "When should students talk?" "What should they talk about?" "Do they have the content knowledge to have informed conversations?" is natural and frustrating when instruction looks different from classroom to classroom.

The ILT, the principal, and the district leader need to have the research base, the instructional vision, and the fortitude to say: "That is a wonderful strategy, and we will go there next. It is so important that we implement it successfully that we need to make sure that the language of instruction is in place so that we know exactly where to use it." Think back to the interviews of the two school leaders at the end of Chapter 1. Both reflect this type of leadership: We will go there when we are ready; at times, implementing one strategy or program means getting rid of another, or putting it on a shelf temporarily.

Moving from Research to Practice

The proverbial rubber meets the road when the conversations turn from research to practice. The following set of discussion questions further the development of key instructional principles that will eventually lead to the adoption of a common framework and language.

Sample Questions

How can lesson design reduce extraneous cognitive load while focusing on essential content?
How do we ensure that the cognitive load is appropriate for students?
What lesson design elements can be employed to simplify complex tasks without diluting the learning objectives?
What steps can teachers take to chunk content and prevent overload on working memory?
Why is it important to emphasize key concepts at the beginning and end of a lesson or instructional sequence, and how should that impact lesson design?
What steps can be taken to break and organize content into logical and digestible chunks? How can that be built into lesson plans?
What is the role of clear modeling in procedural (process-based) lessons? What is the role of clear modeling in declarative (knowledge-based) lessons?
How can guided practice bridge the gap between instruction and student independent work?
What does an effective gradual release look like?
What types of formative assessments can be embedded to support continual practice and checking for understanding?
How can we effectively embed communication and collaboration skills within academic content?
How can we integrate critical thinking exercises into daily instruction, encouraging students to analyze, evaluate, and apply knowledge?
What role does repetition play in long-term memory and retrieval, and how can we build spaced repetition into our practices?

After the team has had time to discuss and reflect on common themes that emerged from their discussions, recurring ideas and key phrases will help lead to a first draft of a set of core instructional principles. These should align with the instructional vision and the research. It is important at this point to be able to say no, and to build from what is known through research, not necessarily what is practiced, to avoid a watered-down set of principles that don't really drive instruction. Remember, the goal is consensus, not unanimity.

The table below outlines an example of what a district might adopt as its core instructional principles—again, grounded in the instructional vision.

Example Core Instructional Principles

Daily lesson instruction should be standards-based and clearly structured with a stated and written learning objective that matches student practice at the end of the learning episode.
Lessons should be organized with primacy/recency and cognitive load in mind when developing content.
Lessons will include modeling and a gradual release of responsibility to students.
Instruction should be "chunked" in a way that lessons can be completed in appropriate learning blocks of time, such as forty to fifty minutes for adolescents.
Checking for understanding must be authentic and provide actionable data.
Instruction should overtly integrate the development of durable skills, such as communication, collaboration, and critical thinking, to prepare students for success beyond school.
Deliberate retrieval of learning should be a daily component of a learning block.
Teachers are the most valuable resource in a classroom, and instructional technology should be used to augment, not supplant, human, interactive instruction.

Once core instructional principles have been developed, the team should discuss how they will be applied across grade levels and content areas, developing implementation strategies and a plan for training the entire district. The professional development plan should focus on training teachers to understand this new learning and allow for process, practice, and feedback time. This plan should include assigning and designating roles and responsibilities for district leaders, administrators, and teachers to implement these strategies, allowing for ongoing support and resources.

Conclusion

In his seminal work on food in the United States, Omnivore's Dilemma, author and researcher Michael Pollan asserts that the reason Americans swing from diet fad to diet fad every few years, like a pendulum, is that the United States does not have an ingrained, long-standing cuisine history of its own.[26] People who do have that history are not as likely to be swayed by the next fad that comes along, because their beliefs about what is good to eat do not vacillate so easily. The cuisine of the United States, in contrast, is the varied potluck of an immigrant nation, with regional adaptations muddied by national chains, ultra-processed foods, and a vast industrial food complex that produces more of certain commodities than can be consumed by our population.

A parallel can easily be drawn to the teaching profession. The massive swings in instructional practices are not grounded in a core set of operant beliefs, so school systems swing from transitory fad to transitory fad. Whether the fad be technology and individualized programs, specific strategies, a new book, or a set of practices taken in isolation, the search for an elusive magic bullet tends to hold sway as a guiding principle. A vast educational technology and publishing complex produces more content annually than can be thoughtfully implemented, and so the pendulum persists.

Without a common understanding of instruction, without an instructional vision driven by a district's core values, and without an instructional framework reflective of core instructional principles, this will continue to be the case.

Let's review the four core reasons why our profession's language of instruction tends to be a patchwork quilt. There are steps and actionable processes that can be implemented at the school or district level to counteract each of these factors, but none are easy or quick:

1. **There is no agreed-upon body of work upon which instructional practices rest or can be traced back to**

Step: Develop a body of knowledge that everyone with a role to play in instruction is steeped in through book studies, staff meetings, and ongoing professional development. This body of knowledge should, at a minimum, include texts, articles, and videos on the following topics:

» The specific instructional framework adopted by the ILT as part of its process
» Science of learning, including primacy recency, cognitive load, and retrieval practice
» Impact of screen time on students' mental health and cognitive skills

For administrators and instructional coaches, additional reading such as Alexander Platt's *The Skillful Leader* and Gene Tavernetti's *Maximizing the Impact of Coaching Cycles* will help develop the effectiveness of feedback.[27,28]

2. **There is little consistency in the content or quality of teacher preparation programs**

Step: Each new teacher brought into the system is placed on a learning management system that ensures that during their first three years of service, they will receive all of the same professional development that established colleagues received, to bring their knowledge base to a similar level, ensuring coherence of instructional language. To allow this to happen, new teachers are provided vetted lesson plans that have previously been proven effective, so they can focus on developing their lesson delivery and classroom management skills and acquiring the common language.

3. **Scattered implementation of professional development**

Step: The professional development plan developed by the ILT in order to develop a common language of instruction is gradually broadened to include other areas that the ILT has decided need to be developed. The professional development plan continues to adhere to the instructional vision, and new offerings must align with the adopted framework and the core instructional principles.

4. **The classroom doors are rarely breached.**

Step: Make Lesson Studies and Instructional Rounds, as well as lesson video analysis and coaching, a core component of professional development and the evaluation process. As City, Elmore et al note in *Instructional Rounds in Education*:

> "Repeatedly, district and school practitioners tell us that one of the greatest barriers to school improvement is the lack of an agreed-upon definition of what high-quality instruction looks like..." The implementation of lesson studies or instructional rounds helps to develop a "collaborative, inquiry-based culture that shatters the norms of isolation" prevalent in our profession.[29]

Plainly said, theory without practice is mere philosophy. To truly get past the lack of agreed-upon definitions and enact a common instructional framework, the hard work of observing, discussing, disagreeing, and eventually arriving at a consensus can only be achieved by opening classroom doors.

A Filter for our Classrooms

The work described above is arduous. Depending on where a district is starting, it can take anywhere from two years to five years to arrive at a vision (the first, necessary step), form an ILT, complete the necessary research, determine core instructional principles, adopt an instructional framework, provide the necessary professional development, implement instructional rounds, and develop learning management systems to ensure that new teachers and administrators merge into the system fluidly. And that is just the implementation. The maintenance takes vigilance, consistency, and resolve through leadership changes, retirements, board elections, etc. It is painfully difficult work.

In the section of his book on the organic food movement, Michael Pollan interviewed a farmer who was one of the founding fathers of the movement in the U.S. The farmer discussed how true believers might talk about fellowship and connection to the earth, and doing the hard work of being cognizant of what and how one eats, but to most others, "it's just lunch, man...it's just lunch."[30] In schools, it really might be easier to turn the students on to Chromebooks and let the platforms do the instruction, or at the very least let AI plan the lessons and student practice. But where would that get a school or district? Where many are now: individualized instruction in isolation, the opposite of what research shows effective schools and districts do, and the opposite of what our students are telling us they need, both through their actions and their falling achievement levels.

An instructional vision and its corresponding core principles and language of instruction should be the prism through which a district sees its work. It is the filter that determines what comes into the school building, in the classroom, and what doesn't. In an era in which, to borrow a parallel from Pollan one last time, the commodity of ed tech programs and platforms pour out faster than they can be consumed, districts need the framework and agreed-upon language of instruction to serve as the filter that stops the gorging and helps teachers find a balance between the human and the hardware.

Chapter 4
The Instructional Vision
Guides the Tech Use

Filter: A device, material, or process that separates substances or signals, allowing some to pass through while blocking others, based on desired characteristics

Friction: Resistance of various types between competing forces, affecting relative motion or speed

Opportunity Cost: The value of the next-best alternative that is given up when a decision is made, reflecting the scarcity of resources like time

When the Limiting Factor was Physical Space

Imagine you are visiting Ms. O'Neill's 4th-grade classroom in the early part of this century, not that long ago really. Pay special attention to the technological tools around the room. In the upper right-hand corner, there is a large television mounted against the wall. Under the television is a DVD player that also has VHS capabilities. Along the back wall, there are three bulky, aqua colored Apple iMac G3s. Near the center front of the room, on a small cart, is a projector to which the teacher can run a long VGA cable with a blue rectangular head and two small screws. Plugged into the teacher's desktop computer is a small speaker using an aux cable, and the other end of the VGA cable. A student has the job that week of sitting at the teacher's desk and pressing the forward tab to advance the images or slides on the projector. On the wall hangs a clipboard with a sign-up list for students who want to use the computers' online encyclopedias for research, or to take home one of the classroom's old stacks of portable word processors to type the final draft of a paper.

Right then, the school's tech guy walks through the door and happily announces that he just received six new desktop computers, purchased using funds from the recently passed No Child Left Behind Act (NCLB), and that he is bringing them in tomorrow. As Ms. O'Neill opens her mouth to object, he tells her not to worry because the new internet cable drops in each classroom ensure that there will be enough access for all the computers. Unfortunately, the three iMacs will have to go. The only hiccup is that the internet hub where the new drops are is along the wall occupied by a shelf holding encyclopedias and dictionaries, so those will have to go as well, to make sure the Ethernet connections can reach the computers.

When Ms. O'Neill goes to talk to her principal, she is told that there isn't anything that can be done. Because of the new NCLB legislation, accountability is at an all-time high, and so refusing the learning tools being purchased isn't an option. Besides, the children are digital natives, so the encyclopedias and dictionaries are obsolete anyway. Ms. O'Neill asks, "But are they really learning tools if we haven't received training on how to use them effectively? It seems like most of us use them for reports and word processing, and that's about it. And not only do I need to give up my bookshelf, but my reading corner is also lost, so kids don't have a quiet place to read anymore." The principal responds that students will be able to access online books and that, soon, even textbooks may disappear.

Over the course of the next few years, the pattern repeats itself. New computers are brought in, and some of the old furniture, books, and globes are moved out to make space, until a sort of stasis is reached: there is no more room to add new computers. If anything new comes in, one of the old ones must go out. So, the first limiting factor in the rush to get students in front of a screen is a physical one- there simply isn't more room.

Soon, though, the physical space limitation goes away. Rolling computer carts carrying class sets of laptops or tablets become the norm. An entire cart occupies about the same amount of space as one of the old desktops. Even the desktop on Ms. O'Neill's desk goes away. The limiting factor then becomes not a physical one, but one of connectivity, as the old cable hubs don't offer the bandwidth necessary to have thirty computers per room all connected to the internet simultaneously.

Having the hardware in place helps to usher in the next big digital push in schools in the middle of the 2010s. The near-simultaneous passage of the Every Student Succeeds Act to replace No Child Left Behind, increased funding appropriations through the Federal Communications Commission E-Rate program, and the rush to have students prepared for adaptive computer-based state assessments through tailored, personal learning platforms bring a deluge of funds and urgency. The increased bandwidth helps make Wi-Fi-enabled laptops, such as Google's Chromebooks, a viable, much more affordable option. Soon, every student will have access to a laptop daily, even if "one-to-one" is still more of a goal than a reality in many schools across the country.

At this point, with the physical space, technology hardware, and connectivity issues largely resolved, the last major piece to fall in place is the deluge of software offerings. With nearly limitless capacity, program after program can be loaded or accessed, and tech companies from giants to start-ups are happy to go after slices of the multi-billion-dollar educational technology pie.[1]

The tech guy's role at this point evolves to be more of a software specialist, making sure that programs load properly and quickly. Many even get a new name, "Tech Ed" specialists, who facilitate the process of getting children in front of screens, while also ensuring that content is appropriate and that early privacy laws are followed.

The Broader Digital Immersion

Outside of schools, the broader ecosystem also dramatically changed. By 2014, more than half of American adults owned smartphones, and these hand-held devices replaced the laptop or ancient (it seemed) desktop as the primary method for accessing the internet. So many areas of life changed- made easier, really- by these magical devices. From being able to listen to favorite music or watch favorite TV shows anywhere, anytime, day or night, to buying movie tickets online and booking travel reservations, to banking and navigating streets in unfamiliar cities, screens became our constant companions.

In the blink of an eye, it seemed, our phones became our primary way to conduct commerce, receive information, engage with the world, and experience reality.

One striking example of how rapidly society changed is these two photos of similar events— the election in Rome of Pope Benedict XVI in 2005, and that of Pope Francis in 2013, taken by Associated Press photographers from almost the same vantage point, of, one assumes, many of the same people.[2] Can you spot the difference?

In the context of this change, schools were simply the next target for disruption. Technology, publishing, and entertainment conglomerates were disrupting entire industries. In one generation, video stores, travel agencies, big box retailers, taxis, book stores, and countless other businesses went from healthy to on life support or extinction.

In this environment that enveloped them, schools needed to similarly adapt or risk obsolescence. Pressure came from all sides—policy makers, school boards, and families. In fact, many of the teachers we interviewed described a growing angst among parents at more affluent schools, at the time, stating that they were scared of their children being left behind in the tech revolution. Many of the same families who, after the pandemic, would want their younger children off screens were demanding more digital exposure in the middle of the 2010s for their older children.

Schools also faced pressure from the new assessments brought on by Common Core and by media reports that breathlessly reported the new skill sets that students would need in order to succeed in the future. School board members and superintendents were concerned about their schools and districts being left behind by the technology adoption curve. The 2015 OECD (Organisation for Economic Co-Operation and Development) results of computer-based assessments (PISA: Programme for International Student Assessment), reported on September 15 of that year, showed that students in some countries had done better on the computer than on comparable traditional paper and pencil assessments, and fed the growing fear of a "digital divide." [3]

The Pace of Adoption

The adoption curve of digital technology was incredibly accelerated. A graph of how quickly computers, the internet, and cell phones reached an early majority of users is shown on the next page, with more detailed graphs available on the book's online notes section: schoolsnext.org/digital-captives-notes.

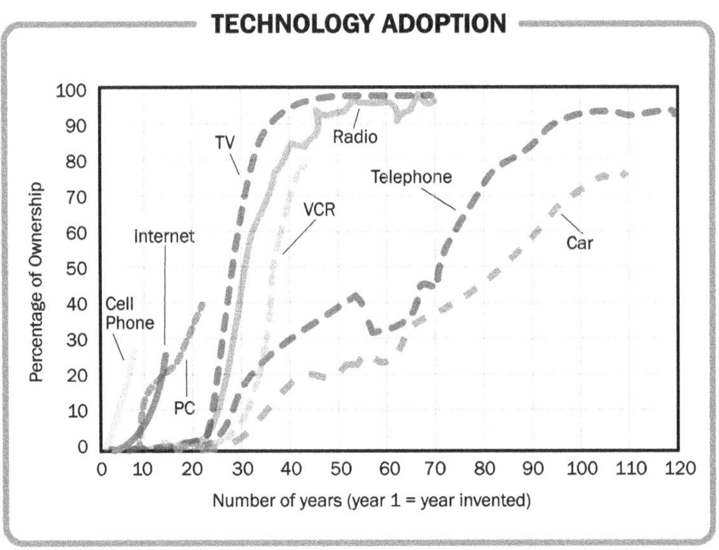

The graph shows that while other technology innovations of the 20th century took at least 25 years after invention to reach even 10% of users, the digital tools of the 21st century reached that number almost immediately, with no ramp-up time.[4]

That almost immediate adoption did not allow time for the change to be assimilated and actually flooded the system in a way that overwhelmed any efforts to slow it down. In order to better grasp this, it is instructive to compare with the gradual adoption of earlier innovations.

Most technological advances began as luxuries, improvements in convenience or utility. As the advances became accepted and utilized by more people, they moved from being accepted to expected. Technological advances moved from novelty to necessity to ultimately becoming part of the infrastructure.

Nearly all the technology we use without a second thought today began as a luxury. Electric lights, indoor plumbing, microwaves and telephones were not seen as a need, but rather as nice to have. A couple of generations later, the absence of those items became unthinkable.

And with the increased ubiquity of use and production at scale, the technology became less and less expensive, leading to further adoption.

This pattern of technological adoption followed a similar path in schools. Initially, educational movies were viewed as a luxury, as a treat. A school might have a single 16mm projector shared by an entire school and rolled from classroom to classroom. The development of the personal computer followed a similar path. When digital technology was acknowledged to be useful and then important to the education of students, schools supplied each classroom with a single computer. Students were allowed to "play" on the computer as a reward in early grades. In later grades, students might earn the opportunity to use the computer's word processing ability.

By the 1990s it became very common to have a computer lab, a room devoted to housing enough individual computers to accommodate an entire classroom of students. Classrooms were assigned computer lab time just as previous classes had been assigned library time.

As technology companies advanced to improve the delivery of services to schools, schools were forced to upgrade their technology as prior purchases either became obsolete or their existing hardware and software could not be serviced and maintained. Whether it was unintentional or designed obsolescence, systems needed to be constantly upgraded.

Processes of adoption were modified to address those advances. It is early in this time period that the seed took hold of continual upgrading without questioning. As computers became ubiquitous in a quickening world, it became unthinkable not to have them in classrooms, just as it had become unthinkable not to have electricity or indoor plumbing a few generations before.

Different than indoor plumbing, electricity, or other innovations, though, an individual or a school's lack of connectivity impacted their perceived productivity. Whereas in the past your neighbor's new toaster didn't care whether you had a toaster in your house or not, or indoor plumbing, or a color television, it did matter to your neighbor's computer whether your school or home was connected and had access to the same information superhighway. Otherwise, your neighbor couldn't email or video-chat you, or you couldn't collaborate on a document. Not having the same level of connectivity meant being left behind. The pace of the change was fueled, as much as it was by new technology and incredible innovation, by social factors.

As early as 2005, Thomas Friedman wrote about the pace of change and how quickly the "flattening" of the earth meant that innovation was overtaking our systems of assimilation.[5] That flattening, and the ability to exchange information and find cheaper sources of labor, accelerated the removal of any slowdowns in the process, or friction. Previous sources of friction for earlier innovations—cost, portability, ubiquity, and infrastructure— were smoothed out, making the technology available to almost everyone, all the time. By the nature of the invention, the world became smaller, which sped the process up significantly. This was different than the adoption and growth processes of other major innovations of the Industrial Revolution. When cars or trains were invented, for example, they still needed roads built and tracks laid to be fully functional and reach a broader proportion of the population. There was a natural friction in place that allowed adoption to grow at a pace that didn't overwhelm, but gradually replace existing technologies. When the information superhighway was built, though, and costs came down, all that was needed was drivers to fill it.

> By the nature of the invention, the world became smaller, which sped the process up significantly.

A Process for Rapid Adoption Rather than a Filter for Decision Making

School technology use exploded as a response to the rapidly evolving environment. The world had changed so dramatically outside that what was going on inside seemed tame and measured by comparison. Potential natural filters to adopt and buy and upgrade and adopt and buy more and upgrade again were washed away, and instead, a process for rapid adoption took root.

What followed was a deluge of online platforms, programs, and applications. Districts adopted or streamlined processes for purchasing and delivering platforms and programs to classrooms. Designed to be as seamless or frictionless as possible, the processes focused on mandatory student privacy laws, cost, required training, maintenance and support, ease of integration, and compatibility. Absent, though, was a key question:

What is the opportunity cost for children?

By adopting this new program or platform, what was given up? If students in a high school Spanish class, for example, turned to a screen for their dialogue practice, rather than to each other, what skills were displaced? Did the potentially improved feedback the student received from speaking to a computer outweigh what was lost? And what was being lost? The ability to look at the person you are speaking to in the eye, the ability to be okay with being slightly embarrassed, and the ability to laugh at your mistakes.

Without painting an overly idealistic picture of the quality of classroom instruction and interactions before the digital deluge, it is reasonable to ask if that loss of social connection was a consideration in thousands of schools, making hundreds of thousands of instructional choices between 2015 and 2020. By choosing this digital option, what personal, social, or learning skills that had previously been practiced get set aside unknowingly? What was the cost of this new opportunity? What was the cost of artificial intelligence writing a summary for a student, or in an instant breaking down the complex arguments of a nuanced, argumentative essay?

Imagine if that single personal interaction in one Spanish class of one school day of one year is replaced by a screen in ten thousand such interactions over the twelve or thirteen years of a child's schooling. And that is going on in the context of what is going on outside of school, where students spend more and more of their time isolated on their phones. What is the impact on social development and mental health? What role does each of these displaced interactions play in the development of an empathetic, mature adult?

Or imagine if the AI just takes over the task of summarizing and distilling complex arguments for students. What is the impact of that on their cognitive and sub-cognitive skills?[6] While the questions might seem alarmist, consider how long it took to make the memorization of telephone numbers obsolete. One generation? Less?

From ancillary digital tools to take attendance and lunch count, to brain breaks, to 2-minute exercise videos, to more invasive digital tools that promised, in essence, to repurpose the role of the teacher into a "guide on the side", the encroachment of digital tools into classrooms was widespread and seemingly immediate. As each subject area and every minute of a school day became a potential target for software developers, few outside of sociologists and psychologists in the years before the pandemic raised concerns about how much screen time students were being exposed to.

But the concerns were raised. Twenge's article in *The Atlantic* in September 2017 highlighted youth mental health concerns tied to cell phone usage. A study by a team of researchers published in the April 2017 edition of the Journal of the Association for Consumer Research found that proximity to their personal cell phone diminished "learning, logical reasoning, abstract thought, problem solving, and creativity." [7]

And the concern was not just about the dangers of phones but about the effectiveness of computers as learning tools. An Education Week article in February of 2016 warned that "there remains limited evidence to show that technology and online learning are improving learning outcomes for most students."[8] Studies from 2011 and 2014, cited by Carr in the second edition of *The Shallows* (published in 2020), demonstrated a strong correlation between weaker recall and students believing that content would be retrievable later on a digital device.[9] Students were learning to outsource memorization to their computers, a crucial step in the process of building mental schema for later learning.

If, in the early years of the 21st century, schools were not to blame for being carried along in the flood of technological advancements, by the late 2010s, informed school leaders should have started to slow down adoption processes and ask about the impact of so much screen time on children. Unfortunately, in early 2020, the COVID-19 pandemic swept across the globe and upended any possible questions about the need for screens.

As schools physically closed, the need for virtual school instruction became critical. New technologies were developed, refined, and scaled to allow students to have access to instruction. The advent of "Zoom" classrooms signaled that the delivery of instruction had changed and adapted to meet the challenges of schools whose doors had closed.

The new industry scaled to provide asynchronous learning for students. Students were no longer required to attend a physical school. Students no longer even needed to attend virtual instruction to complete assignments. Students could access their digital portal through one of several providers that managed all their platforms using one password and spend an entire "school" day going from one asynchronous activity to the next. Tech companies were in a race in a vast, now nearly unlimited market, to provide virtual instruction for students. And amid the race to provide personalized instruction, the development of AI as a tool to increase the degree of personalization and the ability to provide real-time feedback to students continued.

So, something new insidiously made its way into our educational systems en masse: educational technology that, if used properly, allowed students to complete lessons without any interaction with an adult or peer. Stated differently and starkly, educational technology was developed that, if used as designed, could exacerbate the problems of social isolation that had been wrought by a pandemic and cell phones and social media outside of school.

The solution to school closures was virtual learning platforms that were sold to districts as not only a stopgap measure to ensure students could continue their studies, but also a glimpse into the future of education itself. Asynchronous learning would provide flexibility in schedules and minimize the importance of teachers and in-person instruction. New technology would allow digital instruction and free teachers from many of the challenges of their job, leading the way to hybrid or blended school experiences, even after a return to normal school operations.

In the midst of a crisis, many decisions about platform adoption were made without the background knowledge or tools required to make thoughtful choices.

And those choices made in 2020 and 2021 have continued to have a reverberating impact into the middle part of the decade. In a Pew Research Center study in 2023, teachers reported between two and four hours daily student use of computers or laptops.[10] Similarly, an article in Education Week in 2023 reported that students in some districts spend up to four hours per day on screens for learning-related activities.[11] Four hours in the context of a six-hour day means that students are spending, in some schools, at least two-thirds of their day looking straight ahead at a screen.

There is no doubt that the promises of educational technology, if used properly, can have profound educational benefits for students and teachers. From differentiated instruction and micro-doses of personalized learning to augmented lessons and management systems, these tools can assist in filling gaps, managing data, and allowing teachers to work with smaller groups of students.

However, the flip side of this promise is that hasty implementation, based on rushed decisions, can result in the adoption of technologies that are misaligned with a district's instructional vision and model, and fill students' days going from one screen to the next.

One assistant superintendent of instruction described how, in his large, urban district, the use of a particular platform was designed for "45 minutes per week in math and 45 minutes per week in ELA. Instead, it's become 45 minutes per day of both."

"Despite the growing emphasis on technology, school leaders often lack the comprehensive understanding and skills required to effectively integrate new digital tools, resulting in inconsistent and sometimes ineffective technology adoption."[12]

The State of Technology in Education
Education Week

A Filter for Decision Making Rather than a Process for Rapid Adoption

To ensure alignment with a district's instructional vision, a process to slow down adoption must be in place. Not having such a process can result in haphazard implementation, aptly captured by this in the description February 2016 Education Week article: "Without a clear picture of how teaching and learning is expected to change..., going 1-to-1 often amounts to a 'spray and pray' approach of distributing many devices and hoping for the best.[13]

As the pandemic and its impacts recede further into history, and the generation of students who were born with the iPhone in 2007 graduate high school, a course correction is necessary. Rather than continuing to adopt platforms and programs that take children away from each other and from their teacher, without considering the opportunity cost, districts need to adopt a system whose default setting is to exclude, rather than adopt.

The burden of proof should be on the new adoption.

A school has students for six hours a day. How valuable must a new program or platform prove itself for it to be worth turning some of those six precious hours over to it?

Compare the speed with which a new platform or program can make its way into classrooms today with the deliberate nature of textbook adoption. When a new textbook series is adopted for a curricular area, on a timed cycle with other curricular areas, a series of stakeholders has a part in the process. Stakeholders meet with various publishers, previewing, winnowing down choices, and soliciting parent and community input. The process makes sure that, even if there isn't universal agreement on which series to adopt, or mistakes are made, there is a broad awareness of the systematic process and the thoughtful choices, and the pros and cons of each offering. In contrast, consider this quote from a high school teacher in a large district in Arizona when asked about the process of adoption of new digital platforms or programs in her district:

> "(I've) approached my admin about it, and depending on what they have going on, it can be easy or hard. I found an app that would detect AI within whatever platform they were answering in, and …. they never responded to me at all, which is frustrating. But then other teachers ask for a game, like a quiz game, and they're like, 'yeah, that sounds great, we'll buy it for the staff.'"

Adopting instructional materials to be used in the classroom should not be as easy as going into a phone's app store and downloading a game. We were recently in an elementary school in a large urban school district, walking through classrooms with district administrators. In one morning of walking through classrooms at a single school, the district administrators counted a dozen student-facing applications that were not district-approved or vetted in any fashion for effectiveness or privacy. The one characteristic they had in common was that they were all taking up student time. Some of the applications required that students' personal information be entered into their portals. The administrators were shocked, but the experience reinforced an observation that we have made while walking into hundreds of classrooms at the elementary, middle, and high school levels since the pandemic: administrators at both the school and district levels frequently underestimate how much time students are spending on screens in their schools.

It is imperative that districts adopt and adhere to an effective decision-making tool that provides for safety and educational guardrails to students' screen experience. A 3 Stage Technology Filter is a set of guiding principles and questions that a school system uses to ensure that its decisions are intentional, thoughtful, sustainable, cost-effective, and aligned with its core values, instructional vision, and instruction program. There is no one correct Technology Filter, but at its core, a useful filter must keep central that the most important relationships in schools are between teachers and students, and students and their peers.

Table 4.1 and Figure 4.2 demonstrate a sample filter and deliberate adoption process

District Filter for Purposeful, Measured Adoption of Student-Facing Technology		
Stage 1: Vision Filter	Stage 2: Adoption Process	Stage 3: Pilot Use and Effectiveness Check
Does it align with the Instructional Vision and Model for Teaching and Learning?	Does it meet privacy, legal, fiscal, and technical requirements for possible adoption?	Does it demonstrate effectiveness in practice that can be replicated and that outweighs the opportunity cost?

With a quick glance at the stages, it immediately becomes apparent that many "filler" apps that might be personal favorites for one or a few teachers will not make it through the process. That is in line with our argument that it has simply been too easy in too many districts to keep adding screen minutes to students' days, which has not produced noticeable benefit but has had negative instructional and social repercussions.

An example of Stage 1 of a district's Technology Filter might look like this:

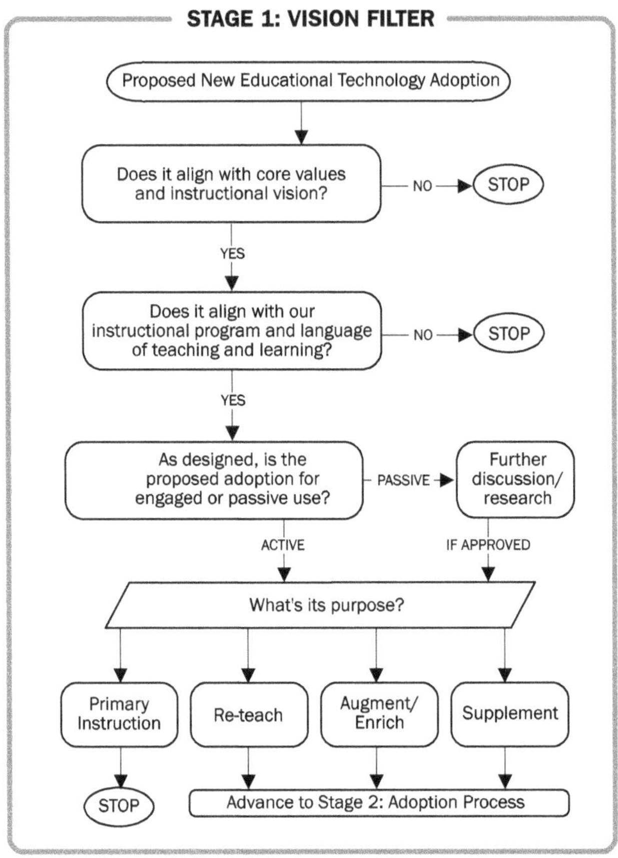

In Stage 1 of this sample process, a new student-facing platform is being proposed for middle-grade math instruction. Through a series of questions, the district decision-making process determines whether to stop the process or continue along the possible path to adoption.

If at any point along Stage 1 there is consensus that there is a misalignment with the district's instructional vision, then the process would stop and the proposed program would not make it through this stage. For example, if a core district value is that students learn to communicate collaboratively in math, and this program has them working independently and not communicating with anyone but an AI chatbot, then the process

116

would stop at the values and vision question. If the district's instructional program and language of teaching and learning values teacher modeling and gradual release of responsibility with checking for understanding, and this program has more of a "guess and check" construct, then the process would stop at that question. In either case, the proposed program would not pass this stage of the filter and make its way to Stage 2.

In this example, let's suppose that when the last set of questions is arrived at, a decision is made that the proposed program cannot be used for primary instruction, but that it might be useful for re-teaching, augmenting, or enriching, or supplementing.

If the party proposing the adoption (for example, a group of teachers, an administrator, or a district math coach) agrees to this limited acceptable use, then the program can move into Stage 2: Adoption Process, which will consider the typical questions of privacy, cost, professional development, compatibility, support, etc.

Once a proposed program has made its way to Stage 2, it will encounter additional sources of friction, possibly slowing down the adoption and preventing unnecessary duplication.
Sample Adoption Process Questions:

» Legal Requirements: Is the program fully compliant with use and privacy laws?
» Efficacy: How well does the program or tool deliver the desired learning outcomes based on the manufacturer's statements or pilots?
» Cost: What financial investment is required to implement this technology-based solution compared to a human alternative? Is it a worthwhile investment for the return?
» Replicability: Can the program be scaled effectively across target populations? Is it adaptable to varying needs?

Assuming the proposed program makes it through the Adoption Process, it then goes to the third and final stage: the Pilot Use and Effectiveness Check. In this stage, volunteer teachers will receive necessary training to pilot implementation and gauge effectiveness. At this stage, a group of teachers and administrators will quantitatively assess the program, with sample questions such as:

» Is it doing what it purports to do?
» If it is costing student interaction time, is the effectiveness it is demonstrating offsetting the cost of that lost time?
» Is there support for multi-lingual users and students with disabilities?
» Does it replicate a program already in place? If so, is this a better alternative?

We shared this proposed process with a recently retired superintendent who said, "Yeah… that's largely not happening. If any of this is happening, it is probably part of the middle step in this. There are questions about cost, compatibility, privacy, and maybe training. But whether it fits into a larger vision? Usually not."

The Need to Slow Down: Introducing Friction into the Process

The concept of "friction" is borrowed from the author Michael Lewis, who dealt with the topic of phone-based gambling in the United States on his podcast.[14] In various episodes, he talked about how easy phone-based gambling became in many states following a Supreme Court decision in 2018 that legalized sports betting. In those states, someone could literally choose to gamble around the clock with no more friction to slow them down than the money in their account and the time it took to get the phone out of their pocket. Contrast that with gambling prior to 2018, when someone who wanted to place a legal bet had to think about going to a Native American casino or Nevada or Atlantic City. With the barriers removed and technological advancements on phone-apps, legal sports betting exploded, from $5 billion in 2018 to $150 billion in 2024.[15] It simply became too easy to re-wire the brain and make it depend on the dopamine rush—"the constant and easy access" as one of Lewis' guests described it.[16]

It has likewise become too easy to have children on screens for the majority of the day, with concerning impacts on the brain's wiring from the "constant and easy access." This is not a book about gambling; this is a book about schools and instruction, and the machines that are now in charge of the instruction in many classrooms. There are, however, cautionary signs to consider in how the brain is impacted by constant screen use and by the compulsion loops that seem to cause similar reactions. Consider these parallels between addictive phone-based gambling and classroom-based screen time, especially in game format:

» Need for increasing intensity to produce the same result
» Need for instant gratification
» Gamification
» Conditioning to constant time-on-device

In her book on gambling addiction, *Addiction by Design*, Natasha Schull interviewed chronic problem gamblers who described a need for increased intensity to match previous highs, whether the intensity be through prolonged play, larger bets, or more elaborate games. Schull described one subject's addiction as "an ongoing cognitive and affective adaptation to upticks in the intensity of machine reinforcement."[17] *An ongoing cognitive and affective adaptation to upticks in the intensity of machine reinforcement:* The more the machine's intensity increased, the more the brain adapted to the new level and needed more.

Compare that with this quote from a first-grade teacher we interviewed:

> "And what we're finding now is that our first graders will not even be entertained or want to be on the iPad unless it's a big, fast-moving thing. The kids will hold their iPad, because they want to show me that they're reading, but they're not. They will say to me constantly, 'Can I just go to the video?'"

Or this 3rd-grade instructor, describing how difficult teaching has become:

> "They want quick action and animation, and here we are trying to keep their attention with a whiteboard and markers."

Finally, this quote from a high school teacher:

> "They're... always wanting instant feedback, instant gratification, instant answers. Before, for example, we would take tests or quizzes on paper, and then take a few days to grade them, and then they would get them back. Now all of our assessments are on Chromebooks. And so, they just have this, like, instant, 'I want my answers, I want to know why I got this score,' or 'I want to know my responses.' And they get frustrated when they don't... get a one-to-one answer. For example, if they did a writing assessment or a speaking assessment that I need to evaluate. They don't necessarily understand [that the feedback won't be immediate]. That you have to, like, look through it and figure it out and read it. It's not just right or wrong. But the grade is actually less important to them than the instant feedback."

Where does this path lead? There is nothing inherently in phone-based gambling, or in some types of individualized screen use generally, that stops or even slows down the practice from getting deeper and wider and more compulsive. The brain is literally rewiring and forming stronger neural pathways each time it engages in specific behaviors.[18] Putting ever more apps on their Chromebooks, to do jobs that human teachers have done for centuries, only serves to deepen those habits.

Research by Daniel Willingham makes the case that screens have not necessarily caused a decrease in attention, despite teachers widely reporting that students' attention stamina has dramatically dropped, finding only a weak association between screen time and attendance regulation. He argues that perhaps students are **choosing** not to pay attention, not because they can't, but because they don't want to. After explaining that a "delay discount rate" is a way of measuring how much value one option has over another before it gets chosen, he states,

"It's possible that the use of digital technologies has changed children's delay discount rates for the worse because instant gratification is such a prominent characteristic of digital activities."[19]

Where does that first-grade teacher go from here? One can envision a cycle of ever more student time on devices with intense game-like instruction and instant gratification, necessitating more student time on screens with similar instruction and instant gratification in second grade in order to achieve the same effect, then in third grade, and so on.

We started this chapter talking about the physical space that was the first "filter" in Ms. O'Neill's classroom to prevent a deluge of computers from taking over the space. In the end, though, the laptops replaced the desktops that had replaced the encyclopedias and dictionaries. The laptops came with a lot more memory and portability, and every student was able to have one. Then the laptops were loaded (not by Ms. O'Neill, though, who had long since left the teaching profession) with a math app, a reading program, a fluency game, an AI tool, an approved messaging app, and a portal to provide secured access to each of them. At that point, the limiting factor was no longer physical space, or hardware, or even software and bandwidth. At that point, the limiting factor was time and a child's mental carrying capacity. There is still only so much time in a six-hour day. And so, something had to give, and it wasn't all those new apps. It was intentional instruction, personal interactions, reading corners, teacher read-alouds, and even fine motor skill practice, because who needs to write when you can type and tap?

What is needed is not more time. It is a proactive filter to slow down—not necessarily stop, but slow down—the influx of each of those programs in order to take a measured approach to adoption and integration, in the context of the instructional vision.

In the educational equivalent of overnight, decades of research on instruction and the benefits of a social classroom have been thrown out and replaced by the unproven promises of countless programs.

Wrap Up

Developing and implementing a technology filter is arduous. It really is easier to allow any program or platform onto screens and let students spend two to four hours of their day interacting with that, rather than with each other or their teacher. But what do schools look like in 2034 in that scenario? Technology use outside of schools is not going to subside. Schools have the choice of giving in to that trend or implementing and maintaining a system that slows the deluge of the last decade.

In one interview with a district-level administrator, she described this process as turning the current model in many districts on its head, going from a "Tech Ed" model to an "Ed Tech" model. Elaborating, she said,

> "What I mean is that for the last decade, our focus has been on how to get the technology into the classroom, so the technology is the driver, and the use is secondary. Now, we are starting to think first about the use—the educational part—and what the new program is taking the place of, before thinking about how to get it into the classroom. That makes for some unhappy principals who want to give their teachers every program they ask for, but it does mean we have a much better idea of what is being used for what purpose, and it allows you to have much more informed conversations. It's been the Wild, Wild West out there."

Chapter 5
Enhancing Teaching and Learning
Through Durable Skills Development

"The only thing certain about the future is its uncertainty. The jobs of the future, and the professional skills needed for them, continue to evolve. So, for students to have the best opportunity to succeed, they need to learn how to learn, how to communicate, and how to think. There's nothing "soft" about these skills - they set the foundation for a mindset of continuous learning that is most needed once they leave school and join a work environment none of us can predict."
– Evan Leybourn, CEO, Business Agility Institute

The Typist Who Couldn't Pivot

In a bustling office building in the 1970s, a woman named Carol sat at her desk in the typing pool. She was the fastest typist on the floor — maybe in the whole company. Her job was to take dictated memos and letters, transcribe them perfectly, and deliver crisp, carbon-copied pages before lunch. She prided herself on speed and precision.

But then, the world started to change.

First came the word processors — no more white-out, no more carbon paper. Then came email. Then dictation software. One by one, the machines learned to do what Carol did — only faster, cheaper, and without lunch breaks.

Carol still typed beautifully, of course. But suddenly, no one needed her to. The job she had mastered was now automated. The very skill that had made her indispensable was now built into a machine.

And the skills she did need—communication, adaptability, collaboration—weren't part of her training. No one had asked her to think strategically, lead meetings, or explain ideas to clients. The assembly line of typists fell silent. And just like that, Carol's job disappeared. Jobs overly dependent on narrow, technical, and perishable skills are vulnerable to automation. Without skills like problem solving, creativity, and emotional intelligence, workers in these roles can't pivot when the world changes, even if they are technically brilliant.

What Skills Do Employers Really Want?

In a study of over 80 million job postings across 22 job sectors, 52.5 million postings demanded non-technical skills. These employers see the value in what have been called "soft skills" and want their employees to enter the workforce with skills in leadership, collaboration, communication, critical thinking, creativity, and growth mindset, to name just a few.

> **Key Research Findings**
>
> - Seven of the ten most requested skills in job postings are Durable Skills
> - Employers seek these skill almost four times (3.8) more frequently than the top five technical or hard skills
> - Demand is greatest in jobs more aligned to the future of work: 91% of Management jobs, 86% of Business Operations jobs, and 81% of Engineering jobs require Durable Skills
> - Jobs at greatest risk of automation in the near term have lower demand for Durable Skills

America Succeeds. 2021. Durable Skills: National Fact Sheet 2021. Accessed November 25, 2024. https://americasucceeds.org/wp-content/uploads/2021/04/AmericaSucceeds-DurableSkills-NationalFactSheet-2021.pdf.

How Can Schools Prepare Students for the Needs of an Uncertain Future?

Over the past two decades, technological tools—both hardware and software—have become deeply embedded in classrooms across America. What began as a gradual integration, fueled by promises of personalized instruction, real-time data for educators, and heightened student engagement, has grown into widespread reliance. Today's classrooms are saturated with devices and digital platforms, from smart boards and Chromebooks to a vast array of educational software.

It's increasingly common to enter a classroom where silence fills the room—students are hidden behind screens and headsets that block out not just noise, but human connection. They are not engaging with their peers or their teacher. Students are presumably engaged in individualized instruction. They are plodding through curricula at their own pace, but little interpersonal engagement transpires. When interaction does occur, it is often technical in nature, how to navigate to the next screen or access an online tool.

With all the time devoted to individualized platforms, we would expect significant improvements in achievement. Yet, the anticipated gains in student learning have largely failed to materialize. Recent data from the National Center for Education Statistics (NCES) reveal that our lowest-performing students are now achieving at historically low levels, with a steady decline beginning around 2010—coinciding with the surge in classroom technology.[2] Meanwhile, high-achieving students have shown little meaningful growth. In short, technology has not proven to be a panacea for boosting academic performance or closing longstanding educational gaps.

Hutson and Ceballos argue that educators should aim to balance the use of technology with meaningful human interaction to provide students with a well-rounded educational experience— one that leverages the innovations brought by the rise of online learning and emerging digital tools.[3] Teachers need to be intentional when designing lessons to use technology to support learning while strategically including abundant opportunities for students to engage in the development of Durable Skills.

The Importance of Durable Skills

Durable skills, as defined by America Succeeds, refer to a set of transferable competencies—such as critical thinking, communication, collaboration, adaptability, and leadership— that remain valuable across a wide range of careers and industries, regardless of technological or economic changes.[4] Unlike technical or job-specific skills, which may become obsolete over time, durable skills equip students with the cognitive and interpersonal tools necessary to navigate complex problems, work effectively with others, and continuously learn in dynamic environments. The teaching of durable skills in public school curricula is increasingly essential if we want to ensure our students are prepared for what the future holds and avoid the predicament Carol fell into. Academic and technical skills alone will no longer suffice.

America Succeeds has defined several vital categories to assist with classifying durable skills. These areas are outlined in the table below:

Durable Skills Categories and Concepts

Category	Essential Skills	Related Concepts	Looks Like
Leadership	Directing efforts, managing teams, decision-making, influencing, and risk management.	Leadership, mentorship, advocacy, project management, thought leadership, and influencing skills.	Motivation, accountability, professionalism, trustworthiness, and reliability.
Character	High motivation, ethical conduct, integrity, accountability, enthusiasm.	Reliability, social skills, tactfulness, trustworthiness.	Professionalism, ethics, and high integrity.
Collaboration	Teamwork, communication, coordinating efforts, virtual teams.	Team-oriented work, team leadership, cooperation, and teamwork in in-person and remote settings.	Team building, team motivation, flexibility, adaptability.
Communication	Information exchange, verbal and written communication, public speaking, negotiation.	Social media communication, persuasive communication, multilingualism, presentations.	Effective listening, social media management, and public relations.
Critical Thinking	Problem-solving, data analysis, troubleshooting, research, prioritization.	Analytical thinking, intellectual curiosity, and complex problem-solving.	Ability to investigate, synthesize information, and make informed decisions.
Metacognition	Self-awareness, personal management, reflection.	Goal-setting, adaptability, time management, strategic planning.	Self-discipline, attention to detail, organizational skills, and focus on continuous improvement.
Mindfulness	Interpersonal and self-awareness, compassion, empathy.	Emotional intelligence, customer relationship management, patience.	Compassion, empathy, calmness under pressure, emotional regulation.

Based on ideas presented in America Succeeds. (2021). Durable skills: National fact sheet 2021. America Succeeds. Retrieved November 25, 2024

The table can assist educators with understanding the complexity of durable skills. It can also help districts identify which skills they want to prioritize. By intentionally teaching durable skills, teachers can help students develop the competencies they need for success in school and beyond. For students to succeed, our schools need to meet the demand for collaborative workers, trusted neighbors, a thoughtful electorate, and creative, problem-solving leaders.

Durable skills are not simply a fad—they play a key role in academic development. In 2011, Durlak, Weissberg, Dymnicki, Taylor, and Schellinger conducted a meta-analysis of 213 studies on social and emotional learning and durable skills, finding that improvements in these areas led to increased academic performance and enhanced competencies such as self-regulation, collaboration, and effective communication.[5] Embedding these skills helped students focus better, engage more deeply, and work better with peers, which in turn improved academic outcomes.

If our Instructional Vision is truly focused on preparing students for long-term success—in school, careers, and life—then we must prioritize the development of durable skills. These skills not only enhance academic achievement but also equip students to thrive in an ever-changing world, making their integration into our Instructional Vision Statement and Annual Goals both timely and necessary.

The development of durable skills should not be seen as an additive to our curricula but a crucially important component of every lesson. Integrating durable and transferable skills into education to equip students to succeed in an increasingly automated world is no longer optional. While educational technology can be isolating, it can also offer meaningful opportunities to communicate and collaborate. In today's classrooms, balancing traditional teaching methods with technology is key to enhancing both learning and durable skills.

Unfortunately, the purposeful instruction of durable skills has been declining in America's classrooms with the rise of individualized screen-based learning. According to a Wainhouse Research report in 2015, "60 % of surveyed educators, parents, and administrators felt schools needed to do a better job preparing students for teamwork.[6] Among the most valued soft skills: problem-solving (96 %) and collaboration (95 %). A January 2022 EdWeek survey found that 80% of educators reported that students' social skills and emotional maturity were "much or somewhat less advanced" compared to pre-pandemic levels, highlighting a decline in soft-skill development exacerbated by COVID-19 disruptions.[7]

A December 2023 article in Learning Curve emphasized that communication, teamwork, adaptability, and emotional intelligence—skills acquired through peer interaction—are in decline.[8]

An Integrated Approach to Teaching Academic and Durable Skills

Durable skills are not bound by grade levels or subject areas. Students develop writing, speaking, and listening skills across all disciplines. Leadership, collaboration, critical thinking, and civic engagement can also be practiced in any content area. Ethical reasoning and character development can be integrated into instruction, and creativity should be encouraged through both subject-specific and cross-curricular projects. Educators should view the development of durable skills not as a separate subject or a designated time during the day, but as a vital part of everyday learning.

Although the influx of technology in educational settings has expanded significantly, it does not inherently promote deeper cognitive engagement, meaningful learning, or enriched interaction. While students frequently utilize digital tools for research, coursework, and online discussions, their participation often remains passive, lacking the personal interaction (either student-to-student or teacher-to-student) that is essential to both deep learning and the development of durable skills. Human interaction creates the space for critical thinking *and* creativity, and is foundational for transformative learning experiences.

By developing lessons that focus on both academic outcomes and durable skills, teachers can help students develop the competencies they need for success in school and beyond. In this way, educators will be taking steps to empower students to adapt, thrive, and lead in today's fast-paced, tech-driven world.

One key lever for increasing durable skills is to include structured student talk protocols throughout lessons and throughout the day.

Structured Student Talk—A Pathway to Durable Skill Development

Durable skills aren't developed in isolation; they require consistent human interaction. In a school setting, this interaction involves teacher-to-student and student-to-student communication. Teachers must create a classroom environment that encourages communication, collaboration, and respectful discourse.

A key component of this approach is a teacher's commitment to modeling the behaviors they want to see in their students. Teachers should use "think-alouds" to demonstrate how they collaborate, reflect, think critically, and solve problems. As educator John Hattie noted in his 2009 synthesis of educational research, these teacher-student interactions are one of the most significant ways to improve student achievement.[9]

To ensure students are prepared to interact respectfully, teachers must also establish and consistently enforce clear behavioral expectations in a compassionate environment. When students have positive models and clear rules, they learn to emulate respectful communication and civil discourse. However, for students to master these skills, they need daily opportunities to practice them. This is where structured student talk comes in.

What is Structured Student Talk?

Structured student talk involves organized, purposeful conversations that promote engagement, collaboration, and critical thinking. Instead of unstructured discussion, teachers provide clear frameworks that guide how students share ideas and respond to others, helping them practice effective communication in a meaningful way. This approach not only supports the development of durable skills but also strengthens content understanding.

Research consistently supports the integration of structured talk into classrooms. The table below summarizes key findings:

Research Review- Structured Student Talk

Source	Findings	Impact
Mercer & Sams, 2006[10]	Structured classroom talk significantly improved problem-solving abilities and academic performance, especially when students explained their reasoning and engaged in debates.	Educators can help students develop cognitive skills necessary for academic success by structuring discussions around problem-solving and critical thinking.
Nystrand, Gamoran, Kachur, & Prendergast, 1997[11]	Structured student talk improved reading comprehension and critical thinking. Active participation in structured discussions led to better academic performance and deeper engagement with content.	Structured student talk encourages deeper engagement with material, boosting comprehension and critical thinking, which contributes to academic achievement.
Johnson & Johnson 1998[12]	Students in structured group discussions and cooperative learning activities showed improved academic outcomes, particularly in math and science. Structured peer interactions also foster durable skills such as leadership, responsibility, and collaboration.	Structured student talk enhances learning by allowing students to articulate their thinking, challenge others' ideas, and learn through discussion.
Zimmerman, N. J.[13]	Structured discussions focusing on analysis, synthesis, and evaluation enhanced critical thinking and academic performance. Argumentation, peer feedback, and collaborative problem-solving were key.	Structured student talk develops higher-order cognitive skills like analysis and synthesis, which are critical for academic success and complex tasks.
Anderson et al, 2011[14]	In STEM settings, students who engaged in structured talk showed improved collaboration and problem-solving skills, which were crucial for tasks like designing experiments or solving engineering problems	Structured student talk in STEM education promotes teamwork, creative thinking, and technical communication, all essential for academic success and real-world applications.

To successfully implement structured student talk, educators should focus on three key components:

» **Clear Expectations:** Students should be given specific goals and roles within the discussion to ensure they remain actively engaged.
» **Framework for Participation:** Use established techniques like "think-pair-share," "talking chips," or "lines of communication" to provide students with a clear and structured format for sharing and responding to ideas.
» **Ongoing Feedback:** Providing students with feedback on their participation helps them understand the material, reflect on their thinking, and improve their communication skills.

By consistently applying these principles, teachers can significantly improve their students' critical thinking and collaboration skills, enhancing their understanding of challenging concepts and preparing them for future success.

There are numerous structured student talk protocols available for educators to implement in the classroom. Teachers should first consider the specific purpose of incorporating a structured student talk routine into their lessons. What learning outcomes are they aiming to achieve? What content knowledge will students be developing, and which durable skills—such as collaboration, critical thinking, or communication—will be fostered through the activity? Additionally, teachers must determine an appropriate time frame for the task. After thoughtfully reflecting on the intended purpose of the student discourse, educators should select a protocol that aligns with their desired instructional goals. A simple internet search can yield a wide variety of student talk routines. The table on the following page highlights a selection of our most frequently used protocols.

Structured Student Talk

	Purpose	Directions
Think, (Write), Pair, Share	This protocol ensures students are practicing academic language.	1. Teacher identifies "pairs" (elbow partners or predetermined partners). 2. Teacher provides a prompt or question. 3. Students "think" and "write." 4. Students "pair" with their partner and "share" their answer, taking turns speaking and listening.
Talking Chips	This protocol ensures all students participate in the discussion equally.	1. Provide all students with an equal number of "chips." 2. Teacher provides the prompt for discussion. 3. Students may speak at any time but must use a chip every time they speak. Once they run out of chips they may only listen. 4. All students must use all their chips.
Give One, Get One, Move On	This allows students to give and get information on a topic.	1. Teacher poses a question or topic that has multiple possible answers (e.g. list all the facts you know about World War II). 2. Students use a note taker to answer the prompt. 3. Students get up and find a partner and give one fact/idea from their list. Each partner shares one idea. 4. At the teacher's signal, students find and new partner and repeat sharing one fact/idea. 5. Repeat multiple rounds based on the prompt. 6. Have students form small groups and discuss what they learned from their classmates.
Numbered Heads Together	This protocol is good for problem solving or responding to questions.	1. Number students off in teams of 4. 2. Teacher presents the problem or question(s). 3. Students put their heads together to come up with solutions or answers. 4. Teacher uses a random tool (spinner or di)) to select a number from 1-4. 5. On each team, the student assigned that number must share their team's response (this can be orally or in writing).
Lines of Communication	This protocol provides multiple opportunities for language production.	1. Teachers poses a prompt or question. 2. Students stand in two equal lines facing each other. 3. Students take turns responding to the prompt with the student directly across from them. 4. At the teacher's signal, students in one line move down one spot and the person without a partner moves to the other end of the line. 5. Repeat multiple rounds based on the prompt.
Talking Stick	This protocol gives each student the opportunity to speak multiple times.	1. Identify an object as the "talking stick." 2. Teacher provides the prompt for discussion. 3. Teacher identifies a student to go first. 4. Only the student with the "talking stick" may speak. 5. Students pass the stick around the group in a clockwise direction. 6. Students can build on someone's idea, agree with or disagree with, or add new information to the discussion. 7. Students may pass only one time. 8. Ensure the group size is commiserate with amount of time provided, so that all students will have multiple times to contribute.

An example of a lesson that has clear academic and durable skills outcomes can be found online at: schoolsnext.org/digital-captives-notes.

PROF as a Framework to Ensure Structured Student Talk is Productive

Rodriguez and Tavernetti developed the acronym PROF in their FAST framework instructional model. This acronym, outlined in the table below can assist educators in creating an effective and easy-to-recall strategy for efficiently implementing any structured student talk protocol in their classrooms.

PROF Framework

		What	**Why**
P	**Parameters**	Directions for the academic task with a clearly stated time frame, and expectations for content specific academic language use.	It clarifies the time students have to complete the work and the scholarly language that is expected to be used during their academic discourse.
R	**Roles**	Tell students what role they will have in the conversation or discussion.	Promotes equity of voice and ensures that all students must be active speakers and listeners.
O	**Opportunities**	Plan multiple opportunities during the lesson for structured conversations.	Ensures that students will be actively processing their learning throughout the lesson. Increases the likelihood of long-term retention.
F	**Frames**	Provide sentence frames, as needed.	Develops academic language through practice and supports language acquisition for English learners.

Some examples of how PROF might be used are provided in Images 5.1 and 5.2.

IMAGE 5.1

A/B Partners

Parameters: I'm going to give you 30 seconds to answer a question about what you just read.

Roles:
- Partner A explain where scientists believe the first Americans came from.
- Partner B explain how ancient people may have traveled to America.

Opportunity: Partner A will go first, then Partner B.

Frames:
- Partner A: _____________ believe/think the _____________________________.
- Partner B: _____________ may have _________ by _________ between _______ and _____________.

IMAGE 5.2

Numbered Heads Together

Parameters: You will have 15 minutes to discuss some of the causes of the American Civil War.

Roles:

- Person 1: Slavery
- Person 2: States' Rights
- Person 3: Economic Differences
- Person 4: The Election of Abraham Lincoln

Opportunity: Each person has 2 minutes to share their understanding of the major cause that matches their number. The teams will then have 7 minutes to clarify their collective understanding and how all the causes converged. Be prepared to share out when called on.

Frames:

- One of the primary causes of the Civil War is ________. Some of the reasons are ________, ________, and ________.
- The Civil War happened because ________. One of the ________ issues was ________. The South wanted ________ because ________, but the North wanted ________ because ________.
- ________ was a major issue for the Civil War, because the South ________. The North opposed this because ________.

Summary Frame:

- The primary causes of the Civil War were ________, ________, ________, and ________ between the ________ and ________. ________ was one of the biggest issues, because the South wanted ________ and the North wanted ________. Another major issue was ________. The South wanted ________ and the North wanted ________. A third issue was ________. The South wanted ________ and the North wanted ________. Another issue that led to the Civil War was ________. The South wanted ________ and the North wanted ________.

Chapter Summary

The purposeful integration of structured student talk is a powerful strategy for cultivating durable skills that support both academic achievement and social development. These skills should not be treated as ancillary, but should be embedded into the daily fabric of instruction. Teachers can facilitate this integration by establishing clear expectations, assigning purposeful roles, and employing varied participation structures—all within a supportive classroom environment that encourages risk-taking and values vulnerability.

Clear expectations are essential for fostering meaningful academic discourse. While scaffolds and accommodations are especially effective for English language learners and students with disabilities, they can benefit all students when aligned with identified areas of need. When thoughtfully implemented, structured student talk not only deepens students' understanding of complex concepts but also strengthens vital interpersonal competencies.

By engaging in rich discourse, students build the content knowledge and durable skills necessary to thrive in an increasingly complex and dynamic world. Instruction that intentionally blends academic learning with human interaction equips students with the lifelong competencies they need to become informed, empathetic, and collaborative individuals—both within and beyond the classroom.

Chapter 6
Broadening the Scope

"And what are the costs to a society of an entire population conditioned to spend so much of their waking lives not in concentration and focus but rather in fragmentary awareness and subject to constant interruption?"[1]
-**Tim Wu,** *The Attention Merchants*

Mainstream public schools in the United States have always operated within and been responsive to the needs of the surrounding environment. From the adoption of an agrarian calendar to accommodate planting and harvesting seasons, to the passage of the National Defense Education Act in 1958 in response to the launching of *Sputnik* by the Soviet Union, to being at the forefront of integration battles in the 1950s to 1970s, to pandemic-era shutdowns, schools have reflected the environment in which they operate.

It is reasonable to argue, though, that schools have never been more impacted by what is going on in society than they are today. What is different now is the way in which societal upheaval is having an unprecedented impact on the actual process of teaching and learning, driven by a digital onslaught that has transformed information, communication, socialization, entertainment, literacy, and attention spans.

To borrow a phrase from Jonathan Haidt, it has never been as easy to harm children's ability to learn on an "industrial scale" as it is today.[2] In 2023, close to half of Americans reported reading zero books.[3] Literacy is quickly following a bifurcated path: adults who can read linearly and sustain focus through long-form reading, and those who have trained themselves to read and consume information in short, bite-sized clips, whether it be posts, videos, or other media.[4] The oldest members of the iPhone generation (which debuted in 2007) will be the parents of kindergarten students entering school by the end of this decade. These new parents are also at the leading edge of a generation that has demonstrated growing concerns with mental health, decreased durable skills, increased isolation, shortened attention spans, and a dramatic drop in long-form reading. The full impact on the children they send to school is difficult to foretell, but not optimistic.

We believe that schools need to strike a balance between the promise of technological innovation and human-based instruction, and to reintegrate the displaced skills that have been unintentionally set aside by the turn towards pervasive time on individualized screens. We have argued against the adoption of technology for technology's sake, and for the adoption of filters that use a discerning, value-based approach to the adoption of new platforms. It is imperative to ask whether the proven value of a new proposed platform, app, or program that puts children in front of screens for more minutes outweighs the negative impact of further isolation and the further diminution of learning-how-to-learn skills. We have argued for a school experience in which children reap the benefits of harnessing technological tools while still participating in face-to-face interaction, guidance and mentoring from adults, and the social development that schools have long offered.

The difference in this chapter is that, in addition to looking at the changes that need to be made and sustained within the school system, we argue that, given the nature of the impact of external factors, school system leaders need to look outside of their systems in more expansive ways than they have before.

The authors all have extensive experience in school reform efforts at the district level. When tasked with supporting a district in its improvement process, the work wasn't easy, but it was fairly well defined and confined. Districts needed to align board policies, curriculum, and instruction, use data wisely, grow leadership and coaching capacities, provide the necessary professional development, and embed systems of monitoring and support. Importantly, those changes were all within the purview of the school district leadership.

Today, the impact of external factors necessitates working in tandem with entities in the youth and educational spheres with whom a school leader can partner, but over whom school districts effectively have little control. Pre-natal and post-natal education providers, pre-schools and child-care centers, local parks and recreation departments, parent education providers, and after-school and summer programs can be part of a broader and deeper response to the digital isolation and cognitive noise that children bring to school.

Schools do not exist on an island, and school leaders realize that the teaching challenges their teachers face result more from the surrounding environment than ever before. Students are in school for approximately 180 days, for about six hours of

> Schools do not exist on an island, and school leaders realize that the teaching challenges their teachers face result more from the surrounding environment than ever before.

instruction per day, or about 1100 hours per year. That's about 12% of the hours in a calendar year. Yet schools are asked to fill holes that have been riven by excessive screen time away from school by social media, gamification, instant gratification, and an undisciplined and muddled use of artificial intelligence, the other 88% of the calendar year. There have always been distractions to the surrounding learning environment, but never have those distractions been so pervasive or impacted cognitive development in the way they do today. The changes to our cognitive ecosphere, in which our children are fully participatory, are so pervasive that they are not even noticed. In his book *The Attention Merchants*, Tim Wu captured the gradual yet profound change:

> "Now, however, most of us carry devices on our bodies that constantly find ways to commercialize the smallest particles of our time and attention. Thus, bit by bit, what was once shocking became normal, until the shape of our lives yielded further and further to the logic of commerce- but gradually enough that we should now find nothing strange about it."[5]

From infancy through college age, the impacts on children are detrimental and quantifiable:

» One study of brain-healthy children of pre school age in the United Kingdom found that children who spent more than one hour of unsupervised screen time per day had white matter that was more disorganized and underdeveloped than children who did not.[6] White matter plays a key role in the brain's communication, as well as executive function and cognitive processing.
» A study in 2020 found that among pre-teens who had access to a smartphone, 60% had access before the age of four.[7]
» Starting as young as the age of one, children are spending more than double the recommended amount of screen time based on age; children between the ages of eight and twelve spend between four and six hours of screen time per day, while teenagers spend between nine and eleven hours per day.[8]
» Each year teenagers spend about 400 fewer hours of friendly face time, about 150 fewer hours of face time with family, and about 300 fewer hours in outside social activities compared to ten years ago.[9]
» Teens' time with friends has decreased by 65% since 2010.[10]
» In the same time frame, high schoolers who often feel lonely increased from 23% to 42%, and the number who said they did not enjoy life was close to 50%.[11]
» The percentage of college students who reported depression doubled to 20% since the 2010's.[12]

Schools alone cannot compensate for what is going on in the surrounding cognitive environment. As educators contemplate the next steps in the evolution of local educational systems and mainstream public schools, it is important that the entire ecosystem around education be actively informed and fully engaged to create sustainable and impactful change that extends beyond classroom walls. A Whole Community approach goes beyond the youth and educational sphere and looks to harness partnerships with community organizations, local colleges, and business leaders, all of whom benefit from quality school systems.

An inclusive instructional vision extends not just to the core competencies that graduating students from that system should be able to demonstrate, but also systematic, ongoing articulation with pre-school and day care providers to ensure that pre-content skills are being promoted and developed as students come into the system at the youngest grades. Experienced kindergarten and first-grade teachers report that age-appropriate developmental traits and skills, such as the ability to follow multi-step directions, communication, focus, attention span, gross and fine motor skills, and collaboration, are in drastic decline compared with ten years earlier. That decline doesn't *happen* in kindergarten and first grade. It *shows up* in kindergarten and first grade, the result of what students have experienced before those grades.

Key Partners in a Whole Community Approach

Pre and Post-Natal Education and Primary Care Physicians

Interviews with health providers revealed that while traditional prenatal care classes focused on subjects such as the labor and delivery process, feeding, changing, and sleep habits, and are well attended by new expectant parents, attendance drops off when the subject turns to child development.

We are not promoting an overbearing state approach to child rearing, but primary grade teachers who were interviewed universally agreed that the visible cognitive changes in incoming students into kinder and first grades were detrimental and that outreach at much earlier ages is necessary. It is imperative that new and young parents understand how easy it is for infants and young children to become addicted to screens, impacting their neural development. The lack of a developed executive function and the dopamine rush that stimulates the brain's reward center facilitate the brain's compulsion to develop a dependence on screens and screen-based games and videos. Stressed and busy parents of young children might be led to believe that educational videos or video storybooks are harmless, but those often become the gateway to more compulsive screen use and a substitute for more personal interaction and the reading of

physical books, especially if the screen use is unsupervised
and lacking in human interaction. One writer described how
"these games prime and then exploit the user's 'compulsion
loop,' an acknowledged behavioral modality linked to addictive
behavior."[13]

A comprehensive pre- and postnatal education program would
shift from care-based education to courses focused on cognitive
development after childbirth. Follow-up well-baby checkups
would include questions and recommendations about the screen
time use of both children and caregivers. It can be argued that
the screen habits of parents and caregivers of young children
are almost as important as those of the children themselves.
Often the reason that a tablet is handed to a toddler is to permit
the adult's own uninterrupted screen time.

With so few adults reading books, relying on harried new
parents to read *Brain Rules for Baby* or *What to Expect the
First Year* isn't a compelling strategy. Rather, short video
clips, podcasts, and pamphlets from trusted sources such as
pediatricians and pediatric nurses can be a broader, more
effective strategy to reach a greater number of new parents.

In essence, parent educators need to reach new parents where
they are with micro-doses of short-form media to convey
important messages. Understanding the impact, for example,
of handing a one-year-old a tablet so she'll stay quiet at a
restaurant versus handing her a tactile toy, might help prevent
habits from developing whose negative effects show up when
the student starts preschool or kindergarten.

For health care systems, partnering in this effort with school
districts and preschool and childcare providers can mean
increased wellness in youngsters, with fewer correlated
symptoms in a few years, such as childhood obesity, myopia,
and depression, all of which have spiked in the last 15 years.[14]

For school systems, receiving incoming 4-year-olds who haven't
already developed an addiction to screens and whose executive
function development hasn't been stunted would allow primary

teachers to do their work without dealing with so much cognitive "noise" that students are currently battling.

Parent Education

Schools have long had a series of events to entice parent
involvement: Back to School and Open House nights, parent-
teacher conferences, concerts and talent shows, volunteering
opportunities, and parent-teacher associations. While numbers
vary depending on the type of event, many studies indicate that
parent participation in school events is decreasing. [15]

Parent education in particular tends to have low attendance,
as parents often feel the information is not relevant or timely
or may be presented at inconvenient times. Perceptive school
leaders who understand that parent participation in the Whole
Community effort to regain balance is critical will attempt to
offer parent education that is:

» Short, relevant
» Convenient
» Practical

Schools can partner with parents to provide educational courses
on social media, technology use in the home, digital literacy,
age-appropriate technology interactions, social skills, human
connectedness, the importance of sleep and social connections,
and other critical areas. These programs can assist parents in
understanding how to support their children in a digital world
and how to develop durable skills even before children enter
their first day of preschool.

In an age of decreasing attention spans, in which adults'
attention spans to single tasks have decreased from 2.5 minutes
in 2003 to forty-seven seconds in 2022, it may not be practical
to expect a large percentage of parents to show up to a series of
classes, each an hour or ninety minutes long.[16] In the same way,
though, that prenatal and post-natal care might be best delivered
in short, bite-sized packages, schools enlisting parents as allies
might also try short social media blasts, videos, and podcasts

to reach parents where they are. In a world in which children spend about four times as many hours with their parents as they do in school, it makes sense to actively partner with parents and to provide them with the necessary tools through practical, relevant parent education.

The most impactful content for parents is content to which they can relate. A series of parent workshops that deal with excessive screen time and the social-emotional, mental, cognitive, and physical impacts on their children can be a powerful way to initiate conversations and change practices that allow unfettered access at home.

Often, parents are not aware of the impact of excessive screen time on their children.

A tool that we use in screen time parent education workshops is the acronym **SMART,** which helps parents synthesize disparate strands of content and provides steps to address the issue of excessive screen time. **SMART** is illustrated in the box below.

SMART realizes that just telling parents to eliminate phones and screens is not practical. But if parents can teach their children that screens are tools, not toys, if they can practice moderation and promote social interaction, and if they can themselves be role models, parents can go a long way towards eliminating the sense of imbalance that many children feel navigating the digital and human worlds.

S: Social Interaction and Sleep

M: Moderation

A: Alternatives

R: Role Models

T: Tools, not toys

A Child's First Reading Teachers

In developing parent education modules about reducing screen time for children, especially those of pre-K age, one frequent question is how to fill the children's time if not in front of a screen.

Research shows that one of the most powerful ways that parents can be a partner with their school is by developing early literacy habits. While it doesn't necessarily require parent education to encourage reading, parents can be active partners in developing reading-rich environments at home. Fostering early literacy skills in youngsters with focused parent education sessions devoted to the subject can be very impactful

Pre-K Students who are read to regularly, whether at home or at school, have heard more than a million more words by the time they start kindergarten than those who have not.[17] Parents who are able to harness songs, rhymes, word play, and games can add to this wealth of language by developing phonemic awareness, fluency, and strong reading habits at home.

Unfortunately, recent longitudinal research shows a dramatic decrease in the amount of time that Americans are reading, with a decline of more than 40% over the last twenty years, and a sustained decline of about 3% per year since 2003. Jill Sonke, one of the study's authors, notes the correlation between time spent on digital devices and the reduction in reading. Most alarmingly, the study found that only about 2% of the respondents reported reading with their children. Sonke described reading as a "low barrier, high impact way" to improve quality of life, adding "When we lose one of the simplest tools in our public health toolkit, it's a serious loss."[18]

> Reading in print by parent and child reinforces core temporal and spatial dimensions in reading, adds important tactile associations in the young reading circuit, and provides the best possible social and emotional interaction.[19]
> **- MaryAnne Wolfe**

A proactive approach to making parents reading partners could include teaching new parents and grandparents simple reading strategies, an overview of the foundational pillars of literacy, and reading challenges, safe places to read, and access to books.

Pre-K and Early Childhood Education

As students begin their school careers, the formative years before Kindergarten play an outsized role in the development of a child. Children rapidly form social and communication skills, pre-reading and numeracy skills, and perceptions about themselves as learners. While the move towards excessive technology and isolated screen time has not been as prevalent in this age group, teachers and administrators who were interviewed reported encountering classrooms of new kindergarten students where the physical act of turning a page in a book was a novelty to some students who were used to swiping pages on a tablet. Other observations included trouble with fine motor skills, pencil grip, and book orientation, which have typically been a part of the pre-school curriculum.

Early childhood education (ECE) is often lumped with day care and does not receive the respect it deserves, as frequent efforts to eliminate Head Start at the federal level demonstrate. But perceptive K-12 school leaders will realize what a powerful ally the programs can be with children in the two-to-five age band. These students are in the formative years right before entering the K-12 system. Leaders should look to partner with ECE leaders and develop high-quality programs articulated with

Children in high quality ECE demonstrate improvements in cognitive skills. These skills prepare them for later success in school, and include vocabulary/literacy, math, reasoning and academic achievement.[21]

the core competencies that will help students thrive when they get to kindergarten.

Extending the Vision Beyond School Hours

Just as Pre-K is critical to the sustainability of a district's instructional vision, so is the ecosystem supported by the schools in the hours "beyond the bell." In many cases, children who attend before and after-school programs and summer programs attend as many hours in those programs as they do in the regular school day. This allows these programs to be valuable touchpoints for student development if implemented properly. After-school and summer programs can embed structured play, peer collaboration, and creative problem-solving to augment the impact of the classroom and help connect students to each other and to adults in a less stressful environment.

Many studies have demonstrated the positive impact of after-school and summer programs. One study that compared students in an after-school and summer program to peers not in the program found that students who regularly participated for two consecutive years had statistically significantly higher grades in math, English, and science.[22]

In many schools and districts, however, the after-school programs are an afterthought. They are often seen as, at best, a service that families rely on, and at worst, a drain on resources, an unwanted mandate that requires that space be shared by the regular school day teachers.

But what if they could be laboratories? What if practices and offerings set aside due to testing pressures during the regular school day could be enveloped in the three or four hours after school and in summer programs?

Those offerings could produce a rich by-product of some of the skills that have been displaced by screens, both during the school day and outside of it. A powerful program can provide connection, collaboration, imagination, competition, citizenship, ownership, communication, and fun. Screen-free after-school and summer programs can offer theater, music, sports, dance, community gardens, hikes, recycling projects, public speaking, geography bees, field trips, new languages, chess, cooking, and volunteering.

Purposeful after-school and summer programs should be articulated within the school system and be a part of the broader ecosystem of what public school entails in a community, not something to the side. Structured, safe programs can be places students look forward to beyond the bell and see them as a place to connect with peers and adults in healthy, fun ways.

Business and community organizations, local colleges and universities

Most school district mission statements include some commentary about the type of citizens they want to produce. These mission statements frequently look outside of what happens in the actual K-12 setting to the community into which it is sending its graduates. Local businesses and community organizations, as well as local colleges and universities, are the recipients of a district's graduates and have a vested interest in strong school systems. Real estate agents, car dealerships, and local chambers of commerce all depend on an educated, striving populace that can work in high-paying employment and own homes.

Unfortunately, in many districts, the involvement of the outside community can be limited to sponsorships of sporting events and "Principal for a Day" type events that play prominently in the local media for a day, but have minimal impact.

An innovative school system leader would look to create and harness relationships that help support many of the initiatives described earlier in this chapter. Some districts or individual schools partner with, for example, local realtors' associations or service organizations. Retired volunteers come to classrooms to serve as reading partners. Early Childhood Education departments at community colleges provide ECE students who can work in after-school or summer programs through federal work study programs.

Unfortunately, these efforts are typically piecemeal and dependent on a dynamic principal, teacher, or community leader to make them happen. When the dynamic leader moves on, the effort fades.

Districts could make business and community partnerships, as well as partnerships with local colleges and universities, a central piece of their mission and instructional vision statements. This way, continuity and awareness of the partnerships are broad and deep.

When working with K-12 districts in small, rural areas, a lack of local businesses with which to partner in work-school relationships, internships, and externships becomes an issue. It is a valid issue that can be alleviated through technology. Many businesses developed work-from-home protocols during the pandemic that could be used now to provide valuable work or internship experience remotely, even in the most far-flung locations.

Some of the challenges cited in the University of Florida reading study cited parents' busy schedules and access to adequate reading materials as barriers to reading with children. To these we can add living in overcrowded apartments where there isn't a quiet space to complete homework, much less to read. Or parents who themselves lack reading skills. Or perhaps lack a sense of self-efficacy in being able to help their children, in some cases due to an inability to communicate with their children because of primary language differences. Local businesses, community groups, and college students could help to bridge all those gaps, but they need to be asked and barriers to participation streamlined.

Steps that a district can take to fully partner with these outside entities:

» Seek the partnerships proactively, before they are needed
» Include community partners in the development or refinement of the district's mission statement to make a common cause

» Establish and communicate the lanes for participation so that each entity can determine how it wants to be involved
    » Financial support or donations of material goods
    » Provide volunteers
    » Provide space
    » Provide work, internship, or shadowing experiences
    » Cross-marketing of district initiatives
» Establish feedback loops and a timeline for revisiting partnerships

The quote below is from Kathy. Kathy was a dynamic teacher in the Midwest who looked for these partnerships for her students, describing one of her experiences.

> "And then you think about how we can prepare them to be successful in a work environment, in that ability to have conversations. Think of problem solving, reading, being a critical thinker, all of that. When they can't have those conversations with people that they work with, people who employ them, and what that looks like, and the effect that has on them... that's something that I don't think should be ignored either. How we fix it, I don't know. For my students, I would have the local Lions group that had a lot of people from the community, and then the Rotary group, which was predominantly men, that I would have come in. They would just read and talk with a lot of my boys, because they sometimes didn't have that male element to model what an appropriate male looks like and sounds like.... And a lot of it, you know, the Rotary guys would say, 'well, Kathy, we didn't get a lot of reading done' and I didn't care, because it was just that ability to look a human in the eye and have that conversation and hear what someone else says, and then have the ability to respond to that in a way would take months and months and months to get going in a regular classroom setting.
>
> ... I don't know, in our schooling and in our education, we have so many things that we have to teach kids, so much that has to be documented and tested.

But the element of just simple conversation and the importance of being an effective and productive adult seems so minor, yet so needed as well."

Kathy recently retired after 37 years of teaching. Will someone take her place, or will this valuable partnership too fade away?

An Ecosystem for Balance

It is impossible to think about schools today without thinking of the context in which they operate. Set against a backdrop of reduced trust in institutions, political and social upheaval, economic instability, fears of artificial intelligence, multiple wars, the specter of school shootings, and coming off a pandemic, mainstream public schools almost seem an antiquated notion. The neighborhood school that students walk to. Instead, every day it seems, a new AI school system is in the news, along with individualized platforms, and declining enrollment in public schools.

But the neighborhood school remains a primary foothold in the upward mobility of the American dream. It is where the children of immigrants attend, and of the working class, and where the children of those who believe in neighborhood schools and public education attend. It is still where most of the nation's children attend, in fact. Even after increases in home schooling, charter schools, parochial schools, micro-schools, private schools and virtual schools, the local neighborhood school still educates more than all of those entities combined.

And schools, and conscientious teachers, try to weave a community, both in the classroom and outside its walls. It is more difficult with students' lack of shared backgrounds and with fragmented experiences amplified by individualized social media, entertainment, and news feeds. It is more difficult with shorter attention spans and dysregulated behavior, less socialization, and more sedentary behavior.

But that is all as it is.

What if instead of reflecting the environment in which they operate, schools exerted their vision onto the community? What if school leaders went outside of the school system and authentically partnered with not just the entities described above but also with political, church, and business leaders, local colleges and universities, and the local parks and recreation department? What if the school district's vision of balancing the digital and personal worlds- the human and the hardware- became a community effort?

Imagine an educational landscape that harnesses the technology of the 21st Century and embeds it thoughtfully into the school day and a student's school career as a series of tools that students learn to use purposefully.

And maybe more importantly, don't think of that student as a student, but rather as an adult who grew up largely molded by the environment in which his brain and social-emotional capacities develop.

What does that adult need during his Pre-K to 12th-grade experience to be the successful adult that Kathy describes, and how can we harness the power of the neighborhood school's community to help provide that?

Epilogue

It is difficult to read the news and be optimistic about the future generally, and about schools' place specifically in the coming decades. When political murders become the subject of social memes within minutes of their occurrence, commentators on television and digital media discuss the lack of empathy in our citizenry. What feels like the daily pulling of loose threads in the weave that makes up our country makes you wonder which thread will be the one that makes the whole thing fall apart. In *Superbloom,* his 2025 follow up to *The Shallows,* Nicholas Carr remembers a time of optimism about the internet and our expanded connections with each other: "... it seemed obvious that all those connections would broaden our minds, enlarge our sympathies, and make the world a nicer place. More communication would mean more understanding."[1] He then goes on to say that it didn't turn out that way.

Digital technology was supposed to free up our brains. We would be able to harness the efficiencies to think deeper and make more connections. It didn't turn out that way either. And the problem isn't the efficiency. The efficiency is good. No one wants to pull out a Thomas Guide paper map to find a location if Google Maps on your phone can navigate you turn by turn, or to divide a six-digit number by a three-digit number using long division when a calculator can do it instantly. The problem is when the efficiency replaces abstract thought, memorization, mental schema, pattern-making, summarizing and the ability to follow the thread of a complex argument. Then it can be said that learning has gone backwards at the individual level. And when that happens at a societal level—when unserious, immediate, superficial thinking is what the efficiencies made time for—it can be said that the society is in decline.

Schools can be a bulwark against that decline, but something similar has happened in schools. Breathless quotes such as "The computer has changed the way we teach" described a better future by comparing an exciting device to a droning lecturer.[2]

It isn't difficult to win an argument using the straw man falla-
cy when the teacher from *Ferris Bueller's Day Off* is on the other
side of the argument. Unfortunately, the efficiencies and results
promised by digital technology have not materialized in improved academic achievement.

The US Department of Education publishes regular reports
on the state of technology education in the nation's schools.
These National Education Technology Plans (NETP) have
demonstrated a gradual erosion of optimism about the use
of technology as an effective learning tool. While the 2010
NETP called for educators to leverage technology to achieve
personalized, engaging, and effective learning for all students,
so that all students had access to high-quality digital learning
opportunities, the 2017 NETP was a bit more realistic. That
report cited the divide between those students who experience
"a school year full of critical media analysis, video and podcast
creation, real-world data collection, connections with remote
content area experts, and authentic opportunities to share their
learning with global audiences" and those who are passive
technology users.[3] In the opening, the director of the Office of
Educational Technology lamented "that most ed tech purchases
are still based on word of mouth rather than the evidence of
effectiveness."[4]

The 2024 NETP cited a survey of more than 41,000 students who
reported that the main ways in which they access technology
are for taking quizzes (84%), creating documents (63%), emailing
teachers (55%), and watching online videos (52%). As the NETP
itself states, these practices, while valid, "reflect technology
as a passive substitution for traditional teaching practices."
These examples are far from the vision of technology as a tool to
engage in creative, productive, lifelong learning.[5]

And so, we are at an inflection point, as individuals, as parents,
in society, and in schools. Continue the road that we are on
or tread a new path. Use the efficiencies that technology has
provided us, by being selective, wise, and in control, to meet
the promises of the first decade of the century, or continue with
unfettered, undisciplined, unexamined use determined by the

algorithms and questionable ethics and motives of technology companies.

But what if schools were the agents of the course correction? What if schools became a haven from the 24-hour distraction we all carry in our pockets, and those practices then flowed out into the community?

Imagine if a school superintendent in a small rural district in upstate New York, or in a medium-sized suburban district in Arizona, or a large urban district in Southern California said this at a school board meeting.

"Good evening. Today, I am joined by the teacher association leader, our mayor, the head of the local parks and recreation department, and several business leaders in the community. We are here because we all share a concern about our students. We worry that they are losing a sense of themselves, that their identity is becoming two-dimensional.

"We are concerned that they are missing out on the development of many critical skills because they are spending too much time with their necks craned down looking at their screens, from age two to twenty-two, both in school and out. And we would like to share our vision with you for what our local schools could be, working proactively and in tandem with every stakeholder who worries and cares about our children and our community.

"Every day, we see a new report about youth mental health concerns, or a lack of connection, or trouble with friendships or securing employment. We are not going to let our schools be a part of the problem, and we actually believe that schools can lead the way out.

"Now we are not advocating for eliminating phones, or screens in schools, or technology generally. We know those reactionary pendulum swings don't work and just breed well-deserved cynicism. Every day in our personal and work lives, each one of us uses the internet, social media, video conferences, artificial intelligence, document sharing platforms, email, online financial transactions, etc. And we know that our students will need all these tools to succeed in most professions in the coming years, so elimination of technology is not an option, but this sense of imbalance we have now is not a sustainable option either.

"We are advocating for screens to not dominate our lives, and specifically, for them to not dominate our children's lives and cognitive development.

"So, we are implementing an instructional vision in our district, developed jointly with the teachers and classified organizations, our educational partners, and parent and student representatives, which flows from our shared core values of empathy, connection, community, collaboration, critical thinking, and ethical behavior. These core values- none of which can be found on screens- and the instructional vision and educational program built around them, will guide our decision-making about how students spend their days, and how they interact. We will reach down to the parents of the youngest children in our community, and out to community partners, sports organizations, parent educators, and others who care about the future of our children and community like we do.

"In our school district, we believe that a child's cognitive, social, and emotional journey begins well before they ever set foot in a classroom, so we are joining with local health partners to ensure that new parent education continues past birth into the critical developmental age band of 0 to 3. We will work with health partners on informing new parents in convenient, digestible ways about the impact of screen time on infants, and on healthy alternatives that help children's cognitive, social, and language development. We know that some social media giants have explored reaching down to attract users as young as the age of 4, and so it is never too early to engage in these conversations with the parents of young children.[6]

"We are likewise partnering with local day care and early childhood education providers so that as students begin that transition into their school careers, they are absorbed into developmentally appropriate screen-free play-based settings.

We know that children learn much about how to navigate the world through play, and that the most critical outcome of this age band is the development of learning, language, social, and other durable skills.

"As students begin kindergarten, they will flow into our 'graduated digital exposure' model, which has strong screen time guidelines by grade level, developed jointly by our teachers and child psychologists.

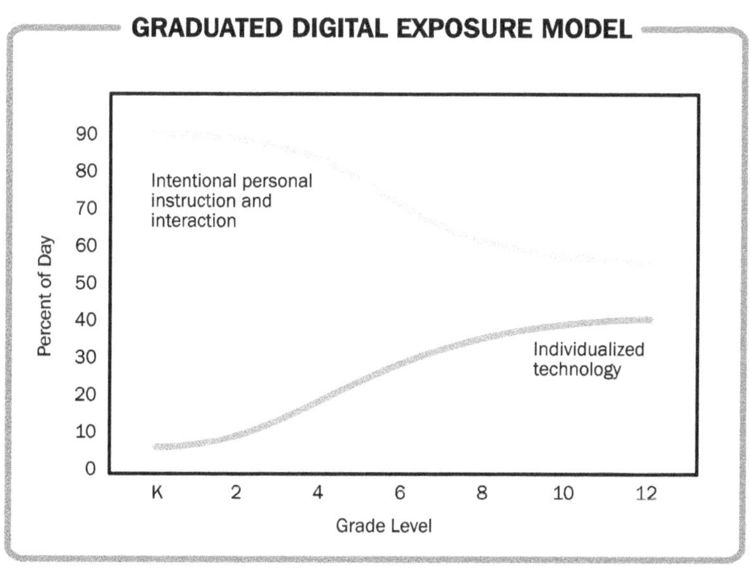

"Children in the primary grades will spend no more than 10% of their day and their week on screens, with intentional, personal instruction being at the core of their learning. As students move into the middle grades of third through sixth, they will gradually move into more screen time in a purposeful way, including some use of individualized screens. By middle and high school, we expect students will be using technology in larger chunks of time as they dig into more complex content, but at no point will staring at a screen constitute more than 40% of a student's time during the school day. And screen time, no matter when it happens, and to what degree, will present opportunities for collaboration, rather than a replacement for interaction, in line with screen usage recommendations by the American Psychological Association and the American Academy of Pediatrics.[7]

"Our after-school and summer programs will follow similar models of minimal screen time, with a core purpose of those programs being to serve as a touchpoint for students, a place where they can connect socially with other children and adults, and to offer enrichment and engagement opportunities that have gradually been lost from the school day.

"As we progress, we know that technological innovation is not going to slow down. Already, the tools we have been given in the educational field- for generating lesson plan ideas, student diagnostics, data analysis, and individualized learning platforms, to name a few- are amazing.

"That said, we all learned from the head-first dive in the years before the Covid pandemic and the years immediately after, that adopting technology for technology's sake can have unforeseen detrimental impacts. So, in addition to developing an instructional vision centered around a common language of personal, intentional instruction, our group also developed a technology filter and guidelines for the use and adoption of artificial intelligence and new platforms and programs. The "filter" will help make sure that the connection between students and their peers, and students and their teachers, stays the central relationship in our schools.

Rather than serving as an "adoption process" which allows most tech platforms and programs into classrooms to further crowd the school day, the filter will serve to stop the steady flow of new programs until the critical question of "And what is being displaced to adopt it?" is answered.

"We know from our collaboration in the development of the vision with our business and higher education partners that the core competencies they are looking for in our graduates do not revolve around technology. We know technology skills are transitory as new technologies develop. Our partners would rather see what they call 'durable skills,' which students carry with them regardless of context. These durable skills include critical thinking, the ability to adapt and learn, communicate well verbally and in writing, work in teams, problem solve, sustain focus, and read deeply for meaning, not just the extraction of information.

A special emphasis in our work around intentional instruction will be the purposeful and specific integration of the development of these durable skills. We can't forget that the surgeon, or the crane operator, or the airline pilot did not learn their highly specialized fields when they were in 3rd grade or in middle school. What they learned at that time was how to learn, so that when they had the requisite knowledge base, at the appropriate time, they could learn the tools of their specific trade. We fool ourselves if we think that the tools of today are exactly the tools of tomorrow.

Just a few years ago, Computer Science was the undergraduate college major growing the most quickly across the country. Who hasn't read about the many computer science majors now who are having a difficult time finding entry-level employment because AI has displaced them? What our students need is the ability to learn, to adapt, and be durable themselves.

"Finally, we know that this vision that we've shared with you will not be sustainable without buy-in from the community. The school day constitutes only 12% of the calendar year for students after all. We know that what happens outside of the school day will have as much impact on students and their cognitive and social development, as well as what happens during it.

So, our team's vision includes a push into the community.

"In the last fifteen years, participation in outside activities and sports has dropped off dramatically. Time with friends and family has dropped as well. And we know that not all good ideas flow down; many bubble up, so we are establishing channels of communication with various community partners, including parent-teacher associations, church youth groups, restaurant owners, and community organizers. We will work with the local parks and recreation department to have deeper outreach into our classrooms to bring more children into outside activities, a key place to socialize outside of the school setting. We will encourage restaurants to take screens off their tables, so that families can have a meal where they talk and look at each other, instead of down at a screen. And we will ask our secondary teachers to not assign online work that is due before the next school day, in order to allow students to unplug when they get home, or to have jobs, or socialize, or practice soccer, without worrying about the assignment due at midnight. The practice of assigning work to be completed and submitted online at midnight, or before the next school day, is residual...but just because we can, doesn't mean we should.

"Will everyone buy in and participate? Of course not. Screens, social media, and the 24-hour tools of distraction that we each willingly carry with us have too much invested to go quietly, and they've burrowed too deeply into too many brains to magically release us from our addictions. But it is possible to imagine communities where a critical mass of constituents—Malcolm Gladwell called it the "magic third"—decide that they want to regain what has been lost by the digital onslaught, that children sitting next to each other at the park looking at their screens rather than playing is not the future they want for their children: alone, together, online.[8] And it is more than possible that teachers want to regain their classrooms because few, if any, went into the profession to watch students looking at screens.

"Each year, a small percentage of students leave our mainstream public schools for online school, or charter or private schools. And each year that makes it more difficult to fund our schools and to attract new teachers.

"Schools can either be captive to the digital environment, or they can create a new environment, one that intelligently blends the best of what we were before the digital onslaught, with all of the tools that we have gained. The path we choose will play a huge role in whether our children are digital natives, able to use the tools but not be controlled by them, or digital captives..."

Now imagine if a superintendent got up and said that and meant it. And put it into action. And if that district and its schools truly evolved into 21st century models: new havens of respite from the digital noise, a place to learn to focus when the world is more distracting than ever, responsive and adaptive to what is going around them, not locked into old routines, willing to adopt new technologies but not being beholden to them, developing students ready to thrive in this brave new world.

Imagine that.

Even old Rip might smile.

Acknowledgements

As with all meaningful learning endeavors, this book could not have been completed without the insight, wisdom, guidance, and encouragement of many family members, friends, and colleagues.

We are deeply grateful to Sandy Brunet, whose experience and energy proved invaluable in shaping the early stages of this work. We also extend our appreciation to Christine Hamlin, a steadfast partner whose thoughtful perspectives enriched the overall focus of the book, particularly the chapter on Instructional Vision. We are thankful for the conversations, insights, and feedback generously offered by Cristy Cuellar-Lezcano, Cynthia Cuprill, Isa DeArmas, Bart Hoffman, Christina Marinelli, Aída Rodriguez, Courtney Smith, Nicole Standing, and Jennifer Stevenson.

We offer our heartfelt thanks to our editor Mark Combes, whose thoughtful and persistent revisions challenged us to refine our thinking and strengthen the clarity and coherence of our work. Thank you to Carl Twisselman, for his patient support with graphic design.

We are indebted to Ryan Nelson and the team at **RISE** School Programs, who have done so much of the behind-the-scenes work that made this project possible. The students that are served by RISE are better for it, and it's our hope that this book further benefits them.

Finally, but certainly not least, we are so grateful to the many educators who shared their honest and at times pained experiences and reflections through both formal and informal interviews. Though we purposefully kept their full names out of the book— from teachers to coaches to principals, directors, and superintendents— their voices resonate throughout these pages, and it is in honor of their dedication to the profession that we undertook this endeavor. Whatever success and audience this book finds would not be the same without their contributions, and we are in their debt.

Notes

Prologue

1. Traci Neal, "Technology in the 2014 Classroom," *Albany Times Union*, August 22, 2014.

Introduction

1. Nicholas Carr, *The Shallows: What the Internet Is Doing to Our Brains*, 2nd ed. (New York: W.W. Norton & Company, 2020), 4.
2. Joanna Brenner, "3% of Americans Use Dial-Up at Home", Pew Research Center, August 21, 2013.
3. Qwest Commercial, Every Movie, 1999, Qwest commercial 1999 - Every Movie.
4. Nicholas Carr, *The Shallows: What the Internet Is Doing to Our Brains*, 2nd ed. (New York: W.W. Norton & Company, 2020).
5. U.S. Department of Education, Office of Special Education and Rehabilitative Services. *Supporting Child and Student Social, Emotional, Behavioral, and Mental Health Needs.* Washington, DC: U.S. Department of Education, 2021.
6. Sandee LaMotte, *Screen Time Linked to Lower Brain Development*, cnn.com, Nov 4, 2019. MRIs show screen time linked to lower brain development in preschoolers | CNN.
7. Simon Kemp, *Digital 2025*: Global Overview Report, *DataReportal*, February 5, 2025.
8. Nicholas Carr, *Superbloom: How Technologies of Connection Tear Us Apart* (New York: W. W. Norton & Company, 2025), 171.
9. National Library of Medicine, *Impacts Cause by the Use of Screens During the COVID-19 Pandemic in Children and Adolescents: An Integrative Review*, National Center for Biotechnology Information, accessed December 18, 2025, www.pmc.ncbi.nlm.nih.gov.
10. Howard Blume, Los Angeles Unified School District website. "Los Angeles Unified Launches Ed, a Pioneering Learning Acceleration AI Platform to Improve Student Achievement," www.lausd.org March 20, 2024.

LAUSD shelves its hyped AI chatbot to help students after collapse of firm that made it. Los Angeles Times July 3, 2024. L.A. Unified shelves new AI chatbot after startup firm collapses - *Los Angeles Times.*

11. National Center for Education Statistics. *Public School Enrollment. The Condition of Education,* U.S. Department of Education, Institute of Education Sciences, 2024, https://nces.ed.gov/programs/coe/indicator/cga.

12. Luona Lin, Kim Parker, and Juliana Menasce Horowitz. "Teachers' Job Satisfaction", In What's It Like to Be a Teacher in America Today? Pew Research Center, April 4, 2024. https://www.pewresearch.org/social-trends/2024/04/04/teachers-job-satisfaction.

13. Johann Hari, *Stolen Focus: Why You Can't Pay Attention—and How to Think Deeply Again.* (New York: Crown, 2022), 10.

14. Ibid., 12.

Chapter 1

1. Claudia Wallis, and Sonia Steptoe, "How to Bring Our Schools Out of the 2oth Century," *Time,* December 10, 2006.

2. Jean M. Twenge, "Have Smartphones Destroyed a Generation?" *The Atlantic,* September 2017.

3. Nicholas Carr, *Superbloom: How Technologies of Connection Tear Us Apart,* 173.

4. Ibid., 173.

5. CMWWire.com and various other reports place the date between 2012 and 2014.

6. Jonathan Haidt, *The Anxious Generation: How the Great Rewiring of Childhood Is Causing an Epidemic of Mental Illness,* (New York: Penguin Press, 2024), 23-24.

7. Johann Hari, *Stolen Focus: Why You Can't Pay Attention—and How to Think Deeply Again,* 30-31.

8. Jade Yeban, Esq., "The Transition From The No Child Left Behind Act to the Every Student Succeeds Act," www.findlaw.com.

9. ASCD. *K-12 Digital Content Report: E-Book and Audiobook Trends for the Classroom and School Library.* (Alexandria, VA: ASCD, 2019).

10. Consumer Affairs, Online High School Statistics 2025 [2024], ConsumerAffairs.com. June 25, 2024, https://www.consumeraffairs.com/education/online-high-school-statistics.html.

11. Jill Anderson, "Where Have All the Students Gone?" Harvard Graduate School of Education. Posted Transcript of Interview with Stanford Economist Thomas Dee, April 7, 2023, www.gse.harvard.edu.

12. Kevin Mahnken, "Pandemic, Politics, Pre-K & More: 12 Charts That Defined Education in 2024," *The 74*, December 15, 2024, www.the74million.org.

13. LeiLani Cauthen, "2022 Administrator and Teacher Digital Transition Survey Reports and Briefings," Learning Leadership Institute, www.thelearningcounsel.com.

14. Emma Kate Fittes, "How Much Time Are Students Spending Using Ed Tech?" *EdWeek Market Brief*, March 1, 2022.

15. Jonathan Haidt, *The Anxious Generation: How the Great Rewiring of Childhood Is Causing an Epidemic of Mental Illness*, 123-125.

16. Emma Kate Fittes, "How Much Time Are Students Spending Using Ed Tech?" *EdWeek Market Brief*, March 1, 2022. Amount of screen usage also documented in classroom observations and in unpublished interviews conducted by the authors.

17. Nicholas Carr, *The Shallows: What the Internet Is Doing to Our Brains*, 123-125, 193-195.

18. Ibid., 21.

19. Ibid., 35.

20. Ibid., 122.

21. Johann Hari, *Stolen Focus: Why You Can't Pay Attention—and How to Think Deeply Again*, 81.

22. Ibid., 82.

23. Jakey Lebwohl, Emma Park, Zach Rausch, "The Achievement Gap We're Not Talking About," July 2029, 2025, *After Babel* Substack.

24. National Center for Education Statistics, www.nces.ed.gov.

25. David Brooks, "Are We Really Willing to Become Dumber?" *New York Times*, July 3 2025 Brooks quotes from a study titled "Your Brain on ChatGPT: Accumulation of Cognitive Debt when Using an AI Assistant for Essay Writing Task."

26. Tim Daly, "Our Schools Have Lost Their Sense of Purpose," Fordham Institute, March 28, 2024, www.fordhaminstitute.org.

27. Ashley Mowreader, "Employers Value Postsecondary Credentials, Durable Skills," *Inside Higher Ed.* September 26, 2025.

28. Mary Harrington, "Thinking is Becoming a Luxury Good," *New York Times.* July 28, 2025, https://www.nytimes.com/2025/07/28/opinion/smartphones-literacy-inequality-democracy.html.

Chapter 2

1. Richard DuFour, and Robert J. Marzano, *Leaders of Learning: How District, School, and Classroom Leaders Improve Student Achievement.* (Bloomington, IN: Solution Tree Press, 2011).

2. Gary Yukl, *Leadership in Organizations,* 8th ed. (Boston: Pearson, 2013).

3. Ibid., 2013.

4. Peter G Northouse, *Leadership: Theory and Practice. 4th ed.* (Thousand Oaks, CA: Sage Publications, 2007).

5. Richard DuFour, and Robert J. Marzano, 2011.

6. Paul Bloomberg, and Barb Pitchford, *Leading Impact Teams: Building a Culture of Efficacy.* (Thousand Oaks, CA: Corwin, 2017).

7. Ibid., 2017.

8. MIT Teaching Systems Lab. n.d. "Stronger Together: Building Distributed Leadership," YouTube video. https://www.youtube.com/watch?v=tvh0xeodWys.

9. Peter G. Northouse, 2007.

10. Gary Yukl, *Leadership in Organizations* 8th ed., (Boston: Pearson, 2013).

11. MIT Teaching Systems Lab. n.d. "Stronger Together: Building Distributed Leadership", YouTube video. https://www.youtube.com/watch?v=tvh0xeodWys.

12. Gary Yukl, *Leadership in Organizations* 8th ed., (Boston: Pearson, 2013).

13. Paul Bloomberg, and Barb Pitchford, *Leading Impact Teams: Building a Culture of Efficacy,* (Thousand Oaks, CA: Corwin, 2017).

14. Gary Yukl, *Leadership in Organizations* 8th ed., (Boston: Pearson, 2013).

15. Paul Bloomberg, and Barb Pitchford, *Leading Impact Teams: Building a Culture of Efficacy,* (Thousand Oaks, CA: Corwin, 2017).

16. Yvonne L. Goddard, Roger D. Goddard, and Megan Tschannen-Moran, "A Theoretical and Empirical Investigation of Teacher Collaboration for School Improvement and Student Achievement in Public Elementary Schools", *Journal of Educational Administration* 109 (4). https://doi.org/10.1177/016146810710900401, 2007.

17. Patrick M. Lencioni, *The Five Dysfunctions of a Team: A Leadership Fable,* (San Francisco: Jossey-Bass, 2002).

18. Patrick Lencioni, *The Advantage: Why Organizational Health Trumps Everything Else in Business,* (San Francisco: Jossey-Bass, 2012).

19. Brené Brown, 2018.

Chapter 3

1. Douglas Adams, and Mark Carwardine, *Last Chance to See,* (New York: Harmony Books, 1990).

2. Marzano Evaluation Center, Condition 1: Supporting a Common Language of Instruction. Supporting a Common Language of Instruction in Education.

3. Douglas Reeves, "The 90-90-90 Schools: A Case Study," Reeves.pdf.

4. Jill Barshay,"The Habits of 7 Highly Effective Schools," *The Hechinger Report*, Sept 30, 2024.

5. Madeline C. Hunter, *Mastery Teaching,* Rev. and updated by Robin Hunter, (Thousand Oaks, CA: Corwin Press, 2004).

6. Gene Tavernetti, *Teach Fast: Focused Adaptable Structured Teaching,* (Melton, Woodbridge: John Catt Educational Ltd, 2022).

7. Douglas Fisher, and Nancy Frey. *Checking for Understanding: Formative Assessment Techniques for Your Classroom,* (Alexandria, VA: Association for Supervision and Curriculum Development, 2007).

8. Marzano Evaluation Center, Condition 1: Supporting a Common Language of Instruction. Supporting a Common Language of Instruction in Education.

9. Gabriela Mottesi, and Mel Wylen. *Guide on Teacher Workforce Credentialing: A Look Into the Initial License Requirements, Diverse Pathways Into the Teaching Profession, and Reciprocity Policies*, (San Francisco: WestEd, January 2025).

10. Eric Jensen, *Teaching with the Brain in Mind*, 2nd ed. (Alexandria, VA: Association for Supervision and Curriculum Development, 2005).

11. David A. Sousa, *How the Brain Learns*, 3rd ed., (Thousand Oaks, CA: Corwin Press, 2006).

12. John Medina, *Brain Rules: 12 Principles for Surviving and Thriving at Work, Home, and School*, (Seattle: Pear Press, 2008).

13. J.M. Healy, *Endangered minds: Why children don't think—and what we can do about it*, (New York: Simon & Schuster, 1999).

14. Marshall McLuhan, *Understanding Media: The Extensions of Man*, 1964.

15. A.H. Johnstone, and F. Percival."Attention Breaks in Lectures." *Education in Chemistry* 13 (2), 1976, 49–50.

16. Gene Tavernetti, *Teach Fast: Focused Adaptable Structured Teaching*, (Melton, Woodbridge: John Catt Educational Ltd, 2022), 19-20.

17. Medina, John. *Brain Rules: 12 Principles for Surviving and Thriving at Work, Home, and School*, (Seattle: Pear Press, 2008).

18. Ibid., 100-101.

19. David A. Sousa, *How the Brain Learns*, 3rd ed., (Thousand Oaks, CA: Corwin Press, 2006).

20. Robert J Marzano, Debra J. Pickering, and Jane E. Pollock, *Classroom Instruction That Works: Research-Based Strategies for Increasing Student Achievement.* (Alexandria, VA: Association for Supervision and Curriculum Development, 2001).

21. Anders Ericsson, and Robert Pool, *Peak: Secrets from the New Science of Expertise.* (Boston: Houghton Mifflin Harcourt, 2016).

22. Robert J. Marzano, Debra J. Pickering, and Jane E. Pollock. *Classroom Instruction That Works: Research-Based Strategies for Increasing Student Achievement.* (Alexandria, VA: Association for Supervision and Curriculum Development, 2001).

23. Barak Rosenshine, The Empirical Support for Direct Instruction, 2012.

24. BedrockLearning.Org, "How Rosenshine's Principles of Instruction Can Be Divided Into 4 Strands," Eve Harding, Oct 11, 2022.

25. Marzano Evaluation Center, "Condition 1: Supporting a Common Language of Instruction," Supporting a Common Language of Instruction in Education.

26. Michael Pollan, *The Omnivore's Dilemma.* (New York: Penguin Press. 2006).

27. Alexander D. Platt, Caroline E. Tripp, Wayne R. Ogden, and Robert G. Fraser. *The Skillful Leader: Confronting Mediocre Teaching,* (Acton, MA: Ready About Press, 2000).

28. Gene Tavernetti, *Maximizing the Impact of Coaching Cycles,* (Melton, Woodbridge: John Catt Educational Ltd, 2023).

29. Elizabeth A City, Richard F. Elmore, Sarah E. Fiarman, and Lee Teitel. *Instructional Rounds in Education: A Network Approach to Improving Teaching and Learning,* Foreword by Andrew Lachman. (Cambridge, MA: Harvard Education Press, 2009).

30. Michael Pollan, *The Omnivore's Dilemma,* (New York: Penguin Press, 2006), 153.

Chapter 4

1. Benjamin Herold, "Technology in Education: An Overview," *Education Week*, February 5, 2016 www.edweek.org.

2. Michael Zhang, "A Starry Sea of Cameras at the Unveiling of Pope Francis," Peta Pixel, March 14, 2013. Attribution in article to AP photographer Luca Bruno for 2005 photograph of Pope Benedict's unveiling and AP photographer Michael Sohn for 2013 photograph of Pope Francis' unveiling.

3. OECD (2015), "Students, Computers and Learning: Making the Connection," PISA,OECD Publishing. http://dx.doi.org/10.1787/9789264239555-en.

4. World Economic Forum. Emerging Technologies: A brief history of technology, published Feb 16, 2018. Can be found at https://www.weforum.org/stories/2018/02/the-rising-speed-of-technological-adoption/. Graph assembled from relevant data from multiple sources, including "Our World in Data" article, which can be found at https://ourworldindata.org/grapher/technology-adoption-by-households-in-the-united-states.

5. Thomas L. Friedman, *The World Is Flat: A Brief History of the Twenty-First Century,* Further updated and expanded ed., Release 3.0. (New York: Picador, 2007).

6. Anastasia Berg, "Why Even Basic AI Use is So Bad for Students," *New York Times,* October 29, 2025.

7. Nicholas Carr, *The Shallows: What the Internet Is Doing to Our Brains,* 2nd ed., 229-230.

8. Benjamin Herold, "Technology in Education: An Overview," *Education Week,* February 5, 2016.

9. Nicholas Carr, *The Shallows: What the Internet Is Doing to Our Brains,* 2nd ed.

10. Pew Research Center. 2023. "The State of Technology in U.S. Public Schools," June 6, 2023, https://www.pewresearch.org/fact-tank/2023/06/06/the-state-of-technology-in- u-s-public-schools/.

11. A. Harris, "How Much Time Do Students Spend on Screens in School?" *Education Week.* https://www.edweek.org/technology/2023/02/01/how- much-time-students-spend-on-screens-in-school/, February 1, 2023.

12. Education Week, "The State of Technology in Education: 2023", Retrieved from https://www.edweek.org, 2023.

13. Benjamin Herold, "Technology in Education: An Overview," Education Week, February 5, 2016.

14. Michael Lewis, "Natasha Schüll on the Antisocial Lure of Gambling," *Against the Rules: The Big Short Companion,* Pushkin Industries, January 28, 2025. Quotes on "friction" at 17:35-18:06. Accessed on Amazon Music.

15. Isaac Rose-Berman, "The Rise of Sports Betting is a Growing Public Health Crisis," *Statwire.Com* First Opinion, November 11, 2025.

16. Michael Lewis, "Natasha Schüll on the Antisocial Lure of Gambling," *Against the Rules: The Big Short Companion,* Pushkin Industries, January 28, 2025. Quotes on "easy and constant access" at 29:07. Accessed on Amazon Music.

17. Natasha Dow Schüll, *Addiction by Design: Machine Gambling in Las Vegas,* (Princeton, NJ: Princeton University Press, 2014).

18. Nicholas Carr, *The Shallows: What the Internet Is Doing to Our Brains,* 2nd ed.

19. Daniel T. Willingham, "Pay Attention, Kid!" *Education Week,* September 9, 2025. https://www.educationnext.org.

Chapter 5

1. America Succeeds, 2021, "Durable Skills: National Fact Sheet 2021", Accessed November 25, 2024. https://americasucceeds. org/wp-content/uploads/2021/04/AmericaSucceeds-DurableSkills-NationalFactSheet-2021.pdf.
2. National Center for Education Statistics (NCES), "Condition of Education 2024," https://nces.ed.gov/pubs2024/2024144.pdf 2024.
3. James Hutson, and Jason Ceballos. n.d. "Rethinking Education in the Age of AI: The Importance of Developing Durable Skills in Industry 4.0," Lindenwood University and Independent Scholar.
1. America Succeeds, 2021, "Durable Skills: National Fact Sheet 2021," Accessed November 25, 2024. https://americasucceeds. org/wp-content/uploads/2021/04/AmericaSucceeds-DurableSkills-NationalFactSheet-2021.pdf.
2. Joseph A. Durlak, Roger P. Weissberg, Allison B. Dymnicki, Rebecca D. Taylor, and Kriston B. Schellinger, "The Impact of Enhancing Students' Social and Emotional Learning: A Meta-analysis of School-based Universal Interventions", *Child Development* 82 (1), 2011, 405–32.
3. Wainhouse Research, 2015, Wainhouse Research Report, https://thejournal.com/articles/2015/04/09/report-schools-should-focus-more-on-soft-skills.aspx.
4. Arianna Prothero, "What's Behind the Falloff in Social-Emotional Learning for Teens," *Education Week*, January 16, 2025, https://www.edweek.org/leadership/whats-behind-the-falloff-in-social-emotional-learning-for-teens/2025/01, 2025.
5. Learning Curve, 2023. "The Hard Facts about Soft Skills," United Federation of Teachers, December 21, 2023. https:// www.uft.org/news/teaching/learning-curve/hard-facts-about-soft-skills.
6. John Hattie, *Visible Learning: A Synthesis of Over 800 Meta-analyses Relating to Achievement,* (New York: Routledge, 2009).
7. Neil Mercer, and Claire Sams, "Teaching Children How to Use Language to Solve Problems," *Language and Education* 20 (6), 2006, 495–508.

8. Martin Nystrand, Adam Gamoran, Robert Kachur, and Catherine Prendergast, "Opening Doors: Understanding the Impact of Instructional Dialogue on Student Achievement," *Research in the Teaching of English* 31 (3), 1997, 220–52.

9. David W. Johnson, and Roger T. Johnson, "Cooperative Learning and the Achievement of Students with Learning Disabilities," Journal of Educational Psychology 90 (1), 1998, 32–37.

10. Nicholas J. Zimmerman, "The Power of Talk: How Words Help Students Learn," The National Association for the Gifted, 2014.

11. Anderson, C., et al. 2011. "Learning through Collaboration: The Role of Classroom Dialogue in STEM Education," *International Journal of Science Education* 33 (8): 1205–34.

Chapter 6

1. Tim Wu, *The Attention Merchants: The Epic Scramble to Get Inside Our Heads,* (New York: Alfred A. Knopf, 2016.)

2. Jonathan Haidt, and Zach Rausch, "Tik Tok is Harming Children at an Industrial Scale," *After Babel* Substack. January 9, 2025. www.afterbabel.com.

3. Mary Harrington, "Thinking is Becoming a Luxury Good." *New York Times*. July 28, 2025. https://www.nytimes.com/2025/07/28/opinion/smartphones-literacy-inequality-democracy.html.

4. Ibid.

5. Tim Wu, *The Attention Merchants: The Epic Scramble to Get Inside Our Heads,* 2016.

6. Sandee LaMotte, "Screen Time Linked to Lower Brain Development," cnn.com, Nov 4, 2019, MRIs show screen time linked to lower brain development in preschoolers | CNN.

7. Brooke Auxier, Monica Anderson, Andrew Perrin, and Erica Turner, "Parenting in the Age of Screens," Pew Research Center, July 28, 2020. www.pewresearch.org.

8. American College of Pediatricians. "Media Use and Screen Time- Its Impact on Children, Adolescents, and Families", May 2020, www.acpeds.org.

9. Nicholas Carr, *Superbloom: How Technologies of Connection Tear Us Apart ,* 171.

10. Kelly Thomas, and Jonathan Haidt, "Screens, Stress and Struggling Kids—Jonathan Haidt Breaks it Down," TEDMEDConversations, April 29, 2025, Accessed on YouTube.

11. Jean M. Twenge, *Generations: The Real Difference between Gen Z, Millenials, Gen X, Boomers and Silents—and What They Mean for America's Future*, (New York, Atria Books, 2023), 393-395.

12. Nicholas Carr, *Superbloom: How Technologies of Connection Tear Us Apart*, 2025: 172.

13. Dan Rockmore,"The Case for Banning Laptops in the Classroom," *The New Yorker*, June 6, 2014. www.newyorker.com.

14. American College of Pediatricians. "Media Use and Screen Time- Its Impact on Children, Adolescents, and Families," May 2020. www.acpeds.org.

15. Daniel Levi, "Breaking Down the School vs. Parents Mentality: Fostering Collaboration for Student Success," School Avoidance Alliance. www.schoolavoidance.org Accessed December 12, 2025.

16. American Psychological Association. "Speaking of Psychology: Why our attention spans are shrinking, with Gloria Mark, PhD.," Episode 225, February 2023, www.apa.org.

17. Jessica Logan, Laura Justice, Melike Yumus and Leydi Johana Chaparro-Moreno, "When Children Are Not Read to at Home: The Million Word Gap," *Journal of Developmental and Behavioral Pediatrics* 40(5), June 2019, 383-386.

18. Bone, Jessica, Feifei Bu, Jill Sonke, and Daisy Fancourt, "The Decline in Reading for Pleasure Over 20 Years of the American Time Use Survey," *iScience*, Cell Press, Volume 28 (9) September 19, 2025, www.cell.com.

19. Maryanne Wolf, Reader, *Come Home: The Reading Brain in a Digital World*, (New York: Harper, 2018).

20. Annie D. Schoch, Cassie S. Gerson, Tamara Halle, and Meg Bredeson, "Children's Learning and Development: Benefits from High-Quality Early Care and Education: A Summary of the Evidence," OPRE Report no. 2023-226. Washington, DC: Office of Planning, Research, and Evaluation, Administration for Children and Families, U.S. Department of Health and Human Services, August 2023.

21. Grant, Jodi. "Expanding Afterschool and Summer Learning to Boost Student Success," *The Journal of the National Association of State Boards of Education* (Standard) 25, no. 1, January 2025.

Epilogue

1. Nicholas Carr, *Superbloom: How Technologies of Connection Tear Us Apart*, 3.
2. Traci Neal, "Technology in the 2014 Classroom." *Albany Times Union*, August 22, 2014.
3. "Reimagining the Role of Technology in Education: 2017," National Technology Plan in Education Update, January 2017 US Department of Education, http://tech.ed.gov.
4. Ibid.
5. Office of Educational Technology, US Department of Education: "A Call to Action for Closing the Digital Access, Design, and Use Divides," 2024 National Educational Technology Plan, US Department of Education.
6. Jonathan Haidt, and Zach Rausch, "Tik Tok is Harming Children at an Industrial Scale," *After Babel* Substack. January 9, 2025. www.afterbabel.com.
7. American Academy of Pediatrics, "Screen Time Guidelines," Center of Excellence, Social Media and Youth Mental Health, last updated May 22, 2025. www.aap.org.
8. Malcom Gladwell, *Revenge of the Tipping Point: Overstories, Superspreaders, and the Rise of Social Engineering*, (New York: Little, Brown and Company, 2024).

Author Biographies

Dr. Francisco Rodriguez

Frank Rodriguez has worked in schools for more than three decades. He entered education in 1993 through a two-year commitment to Teach for America, and thirty years later is still finding it difficult to leave.

With Dr. Gene Tavernetti, he co-developed the FAST framework, a direct instruction teaching model that synthesized and incorporated pedagogical research by Madeline Hunter and others, and the science of learning.

Dr. Rodriguez was a teacher and administrator for twelve years before beginning a career in professional development, where he has since specialized in lesson design, curriculum alignment, and teacher and administrator coaching.

Frank received a master's degree in Bilingual Education from Cal State University Dominguez Hills and a doctorate in Educational Leadership from the University of Southern California. He lives in Southern California with his wife Aida, their three children, two dogs and six chickens.

Dr. Donna Smith

Donna Smith has over thirty years of experience in educational leadership, serving as a teacher leader, assistant principal, principal, director, assistant superintendent, and educational consultant. She has provided strategic guidance to districts and schools in educational leadership and English language development. Her expertise includes systems development, supporting organizations in designing and implementing coherent structures, processes, and practices that lead to sustainable improvement. Her work centers on strengthening leadership capacity while advancing effective, research-based teaching and learning practices.

In 2013, Donna earned her Doctorate in Educational Leadership from the University of Southern California, Rossier School of Education. She is deeply committed to public education as a catalyst for social equity and believes strongly in upholding the dignity of all individuals through high-quality, equitable educational opportunities.

Outside of her professional work, Donna values time with her family, enjoying life with her husband, Gary, adult daughters, and beloved dog.

Dr. Gene Tavernetti

Gene Tavernetti's journey in education began in 1977, encompassing roles as a coach, teacher, counselor, and administrator. His career reached a turning point when he discovered his passion for one-on-one instructional coaching, realizing the profound impact he could make on educators and student learning.

In 2006, Dr. Tavernetti co-founded Total Educational Systems Support (TESS), dedicated to training and coaching thousands of educators. TESS, under Gene's leadership, focuses on teacher-directed instruction, emphasizing engagement strategies, language development, and higher-order thinking skills.

He is the author of two influential books, *Teach FAST: Focused Adaptable Structure Instruction* and *Maximizing the Impact of Coaching Cycles.* Gene also hosts the popular podcast *Better Teaching: Only Stuff That Works.*

Dr. Tavernetti remains actively involved in selected districts, where he continues to train teachers, coaches, and administrators in effective instructional practices. His dedication continues to shape educational practices nationwide. He lives in Central California with his wife, Denise.